CONTENTS

How to use this book

This edition of *The Tempest* has been prepared to provide you with several different kinds of information and guidance.

The introduction

Before the text of the play there is:

- a summary of the plot
- a brief explanation of Shakespeare's texts.

The text and commentary

On each right-hand page you will find the text of the play. On the facing left-hand pages there are three types of support material:

- a summary of the action
- detailed explanations of difficult words, phrases and longer sections of text
- suggestions of points you might find it useful to think about as you read the play.

End-of-act activities

After each act there is a set of activities. These can be tackled as you read the play. Many students, however, may want to leave these until they undertake a second reading. They consist of a number of different activities, including:

Keeping track: straightforward questions directing your attention to the action of the act.

Discussion: topics for small group, or whole group discussion.

Drama: practical drama activities to help you focus on key characters, relationships and situations.

Close study: a detailed exploration of the act, scene by scene and in some cases, line by line.

Themes and imagery: brief guidance on important themes to look for in the imagery of the play.

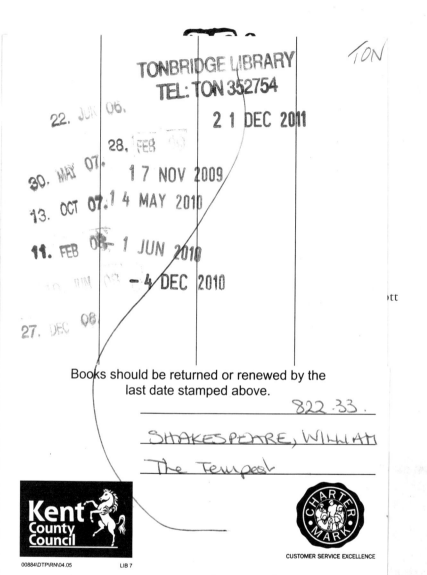

Series Editor: John Seely

Heinemann Educational Publishers
Halley Court, Jordan Hill, Oxford OX2 8EJ
Part of Harcourt Education

Heinemann is a registered trademark of
Harcourt Education Limited

First published in the *Heinemann Shakespeare Plays* series 1997
Second edition 2000

10 9 8 7 6 5

ISBN 0 435 193074

Cover Design by Miller Craig and Cocking

Cover illustration by Nigel Casseldine R. W. A.

Additional typesetting by TechType, Abingdon, Oxon

Printed and bound in Great Britain by Biddles Ltd, King's Lynn, Norfolk

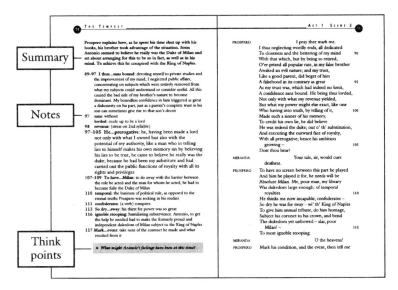

Key scene: a focus on an important scene in the act. This section applies the thinking you have done in CLOSE STUDY to a key scene within the act and encourages you to think about how the scene fits in to the structure of the play as a whole.

Writing: progressive activities throughout the book help you to develop essay writing skills.

Explorations

At the end of the book there are a variety of different items designed to draw together your thoughts and insights about the play as a whole:

- how to approach thinking about the whole play
- work on character
- work on the themes and issues
- work on the language of the play
- guidance on how to tackle practical drama activities
- advice on preparing for an examination
- advice on essay writing
- practice essay questions
- glossary of technical terms.

The plot

Act 1

At sea, in a violent storm, a ship is in imminent danger of running aground. The passengers are **Alonso**, the King of Naples, and the rest of his party, returning to Italy from the wedding of his daughter Claribel to the King of Tunis. They are impatient with the increasingly desperate efforts on the part of the **boatswain** and the **master** to keep the ship turned out to sea. Fear of drowning makes them unpleasant and aggressive. Soon the sailors report that the ship has foundered and is splitting up.

On land **Prospero** and his daughter **Miranda** have been watching the shipwreck. She is very upset at the apparent loss of life, but he is able to assure her that no harm has been done and he has orchestrated the events with her in mind. Removing his magic robe, he settles down to explain matters to her. He says he was once the Duke of Milan, but he became so wrapped up in his studies and his experiments with magic, that at first he was happy to allow his brother **Antonio** to take charge of the administration. Gradually Antonio was able to assume complete control, and his ambition to be the duke grew so strong that he conspired with Alonso, already Prospero's enemy, to have Prospero and the three-year-old Miranda removed for good. They were hustled on to a rotting boat, and, but for the kindness of **Gonzalo**, one of Alonso's councillors, in charge of the exercise, who supplied them with some essentials, they would almost certainly have died.

Providentially they landed on the island, where they have now lived for twelve years. Newly arrived on the island in the now-wrecked ship, are Alonso, his brother **Sebastian** and his son **Ferdinand**, together with Gonzalo and other courtiers. Prospero's usurping brother Antonio is also one of the party. Prospero has recognised that he must seize this moment or he will never prosper.

Miranda has more questions to ask, but Prospero causes her to fall into a deep sleep. He then summons up **Ariel**, a spirit who serves him. Ariel tells Prospero how he managed the storm and the wreck and Prospero says that he intends to make his enemies think they are mad. Ariel caused all but the sailors to abandon ship. They are asleep under hatches in a safe harbour. The rest of the fleet is bound for Naples, thinking their king is dead. The king's party is on the island; Ferdinand is safe also, but is elsewhere, on his own.

Prospero has more work for Ariel, who now demands his liberty. Prospero has to remind him of how he found him imprisoned, howling, in the split trunk of a pine tree. He had been put there for refusing to obey the grosser commands of Sycorax, a witch banished to the island when pregnant. To make Ariel obey, Prospero threatens to imprison him again, then tells him to take on the shape of a sea-nymph and promises him his freedom in two days.

When Miranda wakes, she accompanies Prospero to visit **Caliban** 'a deformed slave', the son of Sycorax, who performs all their menial tasks, and whom they address as 'slave, hag-seed, malice'. Caliban is a grudging and malevolent servant, claiming that they stole the island from him, reducing him from king to slave. Since he attempted to rape Miranda, he has been imprisoned in a rock. They had taught him their language. Now, he says, he can use it to curse them.

Ariel has drawn Ferdinand to Prospero and Miranda, singing of Ferdinand's father, 'drowning' and 'sea-change'. The young prince is convinced his father has drowned and Ariel's strange song seems to confirm this. When Miranda sees the young man she is entranced, and finds it difficult to believe he is a man and not a spirit. Ferdinand is equally impressed with her. Prospero has planned this love at first sight but decides to make Ferdinand's winning of Miranda more difficult, and so more prized.

Suggesting that the young man is a spy seeking to win the island from him, Prospero puts a paralysing spell on him as he protests and tries to resist. Miranda tries to assure Ferdinand that her father is not an ogre. Prospero leads Ariel away to give him further instructions.

Act 2

Gonzalo, pointing out that they have escaped drowning, tries to cheer up Alonso, who is grieving over the loss of his son. Alonso begs him to stop, but Gonzalo doggedly continues, mocked by Sebastian and Antonio. The talk turns to Alonso's 'loss' of his daughter in marriage to the African king of a distant kingdom on the North African coast. **Francisco** claims he saw Ferdinand swimming strongly. Sebastian suddenly attacks Alonso for the marriage he arranged for Claribel. They had tried to dissuade him, he says, and Claribel had only agreed out of duty. To distract Alonso, Gonzalo tells them how he would administer the island. Soon Ariel comes in, invisible to them all, playing music. Apart from Antonio and Sebastian they all fall asleep, Alonso last of all, with the two men promising to guard him while he sleeps.

As soon as Alonso is asleep, Antonio starts to persuade Sebastian that there is not much difference between sleep and death, and that the crown of Naples is there for the grasping. Sebastian gradually understands, remembering how Antonio had achieved his dukedom. They have agreed to kill Alonso and Gonzalo but Ariel wakes up Gonzalo. The two conspirators, swords already drawn, concoct a story about having heard wild animals. They all leave to search for Ferdinand.

Caliban, carrying wood and cursing Prospero, sees a survivor of the wreck approaching, **Trinculo**, a jester. Thinking he is a spirit sent to torment him, Caliban falls flat in the hope that he will not be noticed. There is a storm approaching and Trinculo seeks the only shelter available – under Caliban's coat. **Stephano**, a drunken butler, comes in singing and, hearing Caliban calling out to the spirits not to hurt him, gives the mouth he can see, wine to drink. Trinculo recognises his voice and Stephano is amazed at the two-headed, four-legged creature. Caliban, impressed by the wine, is soon ready to call Stephano king in place of Prospero. Stephano decides to 'inherit' the island.

Act 3

Ferdinand, wearily carrying and piling logs is sustained by
thoughts of Miranda. She comes to see him and offers to help.
Prospero observes this from a distance. They soon declare their
love for each other. Ferdinand reveals that, all too sadly, he is
now a king. They agree to marry. Prospero, still watching and
listening is pleased, but he has more magic to attend to.

In drunken joking between Trinculo and Stephano, Caliban
is seen as 'servant-monster, moon-calf' and has been made
drunk. Ariel, invisible, makes it seem as though Trinculo is
constantly doubting Stephano. This causes a quarrel which is
patched up as Caliban suggests ways and means of killing
Prospero so that Stephano can rule the island in his place. He
knows they must first seize Prospero's books, where his power-
base lies. Caliban tells Stephano about Miranda – they could be
king and queen on the island. Ariel goes to report back to
Prospero.

Alonso and the others have been searching for Ferdinand and
now Gonzalo is too weary to continue. Alonso is ready to
conclude that Ferdinand has drowned. Sebastian and Antonio
are still plotting to murder Alonso. Suddenly strange figures
enter with a banqueting table and food. As they decide to eat,
Ariel, now disguised as the mythological harpy (a creature – half
woman, half bird), claps his wings and the banquet vanishes.
He declares they are unfit to live and have been made mad. He
reminds them of the crime they committed and warns of similar
punishment. Ariel vanishes, and the 'shapes' remove the table.

Congratulating Ariel on his performance, Prospero confirms
that his enemies are now in his power, and goes off to visit
Ferdinand and Miranda. Alonso has begun to be aware of his
guilt and to connect this with the supposed fate of his son. He
seems to hear Prospero's name in sea, wind and thunder and,
feeling that he deserves to die, he leaves. Antonio and Sebastian
rush off, looking for enemies they can fight with swords.
Gonzalo stays behind but sends others after them in the hope
of preventing worse trouble.

Act 4

Prospero apologises to Ferdinand for his treatment of him and is happy to agree to their engagement, stipulating only that Miranda must still be a virgin when she marries him. Ferdinand agrees to this. Prospero tells Ariel to bring some of his spirits to help put on an entertainment for the engaged couple. This proves to be a masque with the goddess of plenty and fertility, **Ceres**, and the queen of the gods and patroness of marriage, **Juno**, calling blessings down on them. Prospero suddenly remembers the conspiracy against his life. The entertainment stops. Prospero calls Ariel who tells him he has led the three drunken conspirators through thorns and brambles into a stinking pond. Prospero decides to distract them with gaudy clothes and trinkets which Ariel hangs on a line. Caliban does not fall for the trick, but the others do. They are hunted off by spirit dogs and hounds after which goblins will torment and hurt them.

Act 5

Ariel reports that the king and his followers are under a spell. Alonso, Sebastian and Antonio seem mad, while Gonzalo weeps at the state they are in. Even Ariel, a spirit, not a human being, is moved. While Ariel goes to fetch them, Prospero solemnly reviews all his magic powers and equally solemnly renounces them. He will break his magic staff and throw his book deep into the sea. Prospero then addresses Gonzalo as the man who saved him and Miranda and promises he shall be rewarded. He accuses Alonso and Sebastian of their cruelty to him and Miranda. He forgives his own brother, but mentions his conspiracy, with Sebastian, to kill Alonso. None of them recognises Prospero, so he sends for his hat and rapier as a means to their recognition of him as the Duke of Milan.

Ariel is sent to bring the boatswain and the ship's master. Meanwhile Alonso gradually emerges from the enchantment and starts to ask questions. Prospero demands the return of his dukedom. Alonso mourns the loss of Ferdinand and Prospero compares it with his 'loss' of Miranda. He reveals Miranda and Ferdinand who are playing chess. Alonso can hardly believe his eyes after the illusions he has seen. He welcomes Miranda as his daughter, confessing that he must beg her forgiveness.

The bewildered boatswain and master arrive to tell how they were released and how their ship is as good as new. Ariel then drives in Caliban, Stephano and Trinculo. Caliban realises how foolish he has been and is sent off to prepare Prospero's cell for the visitors, who are invited to spend the night there before taking ship for Naples. Prospero promises to tell his story.

In an epilogue to the audience, Prospero asks them to send him off to Naples and not to keep him confined on the island. It is also the traditional request for applause and for the audience's indulgence, but he claims that he now lacks all his former powers and must rely on their prayers for pardon, as they themselves hope for mercy.

The text of Shakespeare's plays

Shakespeare's work is generally treated with such immense respect that it may seem strange to admit that we cannot be certain exactly what he wrote. The reasons for this mystery lie in the circumstances of the theatre and publishing in the sixteenth and seventeenth centuries.

Shakespeare was a professional actor and shareholder in a company of actors, the Lord Chamberlain's Men, for whom he wrote his plays. Since copyright and performing rights did not exist before the eighteenth century there was the risk that, if a play was successful, other companies would perform it and reap the financial rewards. To avoid this, acting companies guarded the handwritten copy of a completed work. It was their most valuable resource and was kept by the prompter: each actor was given only his own lines and cues. None of these manuscripts survives to the present day. The lack of printed texts may seem strange but, like the work of other playwrights of his time, Shakespeare's plays existed essentially as oral, not written, texts. His concern was with what they looked and sounded like on stage. However, there was money to be made from printed plays and during his lifetime nearly half of Shakespeare's plays were printed in what are known as quartos: paperback editions of single plays. Some of these, called 'bad' quartos, are pirated editions based on the memories of actors and audience. Others are much more accurate and may have been authorised by Shakespeare or the shareholders in his company, perhaps to capitalize on a popular success which was about to go out of repertory or to forestall a pirate edition. None, however, seems to have been supervised by the playwright and all differ, often considerably, from the key text of Shakespeare's plays, the *First Folio*.

The *First Folio*, published in 1623, is a collected edition of all Shakespeare's plays (with the exception of *Pericles*). It was edited by John Hemming and Henry Condell, two shareholders in the Lord Chamberlain's Men, using 'good' quartos, prompt copies and other company papers to provide an accurate text as a fitting memorial to their partner. They did not start the editing process until after Shakespeare had died and apparently based their editorial decisions on what had happened in the theatre. We cannot be certain how far they represent what Shakespeare's ultimate intentions might have been. Even if Shakespeare had approved the text which went to the printer, it was the custom of writers to leave much of the detail of spelling and punctuation to the printer or to a scribe who made a fair copy from the playwright's rough drafts. The scribe and the printer thus introduced their own interpretations and inaccuracies into the text. The *First Folio* was reprinted three times in the seventeenth century and each edition corrected some inaccuracies and introduced new errors. A modern editor tries to provide a text which is easy to read and close to Shakespeare's presumed intentions. To do this the editor may modernise spelling and change punctuation, add stage directions and scene divisions, and make important decisions about which of several readings in quarto and folio editions is most acceptable. If you are able to compare this edition of the play with other editions, you are likely to find many minor variations between them as well as occasional major differences which could change your view of a character or situation.

Studying the play
A question of approach

When you study a play, you need to be able to see it from two different perspectives simultaneously. You need to be able to imagine and experience the text line by line, sharing the thoughts and feelings of the characters as they go through the events of the play, but at the same time you need to be able to 'look down on' the play as a whole and see the patterns of character and relationship, of language and imagery, of themes and issues.

A play is essentially an audio-visual experience. No two members of the audience see quite the same 'play' and no two performances are ever exactly the same. Two important lessons should be learned from this. The first is that the printed text is not the play; the play is what you see when you go to the theatre. The text is a set of instructions to be interpreted by the director and the actors, artists and technicians. The second lesson is that there is no one 'right answer' to the play, only a range of possible interpretations. Your view can be just as valid as any one else's, but only if you can present it clearly and support it by valid arguments derived from the text. For this purpose you need, again, to see it as a whole and as a set of details.

Thinking about the play

By the time you have discussed the text carefully, you should be beginning to clarify and organize your response to the play as a whole. Most examination questions concentrate on content and form, and these are useful terms which offer you an approach and a framework within which you can prepare to write successfully.

Your first task is to establish clearly in your mind the broad issues raised by the text and the possible areas for discussion, including major characters. You need to consider and discuss some of the possible views and interpretations of these issues and lay down a sensible framework within which personal response can be convincing and well-considered. You also need to get close to the text and identify the key incidents, scenes or even quotations which will form the basis of any essay. When you come to write essays on the whole text, or even a specified passage, the appropriate textual evidence and illustrations should be noted and easily available.

THE TEMPEST

CHARACTERS

ALONSO, King of Naples
SEBASTIAN, his brother
PROSPERO, the right Duke of Milan
ANTONIO, his brother, the usurping DUKE OF MILAN
FERDINAND, son to the King of Naples
GONZALO, an honest old councillor
ADRIAN and FRANCISCO, lords
CALIBAN, a savage and deformed slave
TRINCULO, a jester
STEPHANO, a drunken butler
MASTER OF A SHIP
BOATSWAIN
MARINERS
MIRANDA, daughter to Prospero
ARIEL, an airy spirit
IRIS
CERES
JUNO } spirits
NYMPHS
REAPERS

SCENE *a ship at sea; an uninhabited island*

A ship is in trouble and in danger of running aground in the storm. The master and the boatswain are trying desperately to save the ship and they make it clear that they can do without the presence on deck of the king and his nobles with their nervous instructions.

3 **yarely**: briskly, quickly
bestir: get on with it

6 **Take in the topsail**: this would reduce the area of sail and lessen the speed of the ship
Tend: attend

7 **whistle**: only the master gave instructions by whistle, when the storm drowned out verbal commands
blow...wind: shouted to the storm (compare with 'Blow, winds, and crack your cheeks!' *King Lear* Act 3 scene 2 line 1)
room: the space remaining between ship and shore. 'Searoom' is the space without obstruction in which a ship can be manoeuvred

8–9 **Play the men**: 'ply' may be meant, but the sense is 'set the men on'. An irritating instruction from a non-sailor, especially when it is already being done

12 **mar**: hinder, interrupt
Keep: stay in

15 **Hence**: go away!
cares: a singular verb for a plural subject is quite common in this play
roarers: the roaring waves, with the parallel sense of noisy revellers or riotous men

20–22 **You...more**: you are a member of the king's privy council, if you can make these unruly elements fall silent and bring us peace now, then we can stop work

---

- *How does Gonzalo see his role in all this upheaval?*

Act one

Scene 1

On a ship at sea
A tempestuous noise of thunder and lightning heard
Enter a SHIPMASTER *and a* BOATSWAIN

MASTER	Boatswain!
BOATSWAIN	Here master. What cheer?
MASTER	Good. Speak to the mariners. Fall to 't yarely, or we run ourselves aground. Bestir, bestir. [*Exit*

Enter MARINERS

BOATSWAIN   Heigh my hearts! cheerly, cheerly my hearts!   5
yare, yare! Take in the topsail. Tend to the master's
whistle. Blow till thou burst thy wind, if room enough.

Enter ALONSO, SEBASTIAN, ANTONIO, FERDINAND,
GONZALO, *and others*

ALONSO   Good boatswain have care. Where's the master? Play
the men.

BOATSWAIN   I pray now keep below.   10

ANTONIO   Where is the master, boatswain?

BOATSWAIN   Do you not hear him? You mar our labour. Keep
your cabins. You do assist the storm.

GONZALO   Nay, good, be patient.

BOATSWAIN   When the sea is. Hence! What cares these roarers 15
for the name of king? To cabin. Silence! Trouble us
not.

GONZALO   Good, yet remember whom thou hast aboard.

BOATSWAIN   None that I more love than myself. You are a
councillor; if you can command these elements   20

Gonzalo considers that the boatswain looks more like a case for hanging than drowning in a shipwreck. Meanwhile the seamen are trying to turn the ship around, away from the shore and towards the open sea. Sebastian and Alonso shout at them. Two sailors bring the news that their efforts have failed – it is hopeless.

24 **mischance…hap**: imminent disaster, if this is going to happen

28 **drowning mark**: nothing in his face indicates that he is likely to drown. Gonzalo is trying to convince himself that they are all less likely to die in a shipwreck if the proverb holds true 'If a man be doomed to be hanged, he will never be drowned' **his complexion…gallows**: he looks villainous. He's more likely to hang. 'Complexion' meant 'disposition, temperament' as well as 'appearance'

29–30 **Stand fast…cable**: Fate – don't change your mind about his hanging; make the rope he is to be hanged by, our anchor cable

34 **Bring her…main-course**: heave-to. The aim was, with the aid of the mainsail 'main-course' to have the ship as near stationary as possible, in the hope of riding out the storm

35–36 **They…office**: the passengers are making more noise than the storm or than we make as we work

39 **A pox o'**: curses on

41 **Work you then**: why don't you do the job then?

45 **warrant him for**: guarantee him against

46-47 **an unstanched wench**: a menstruating woman ('unstanched' means the flow has not been stopped)

48 **a-hold**: close to the wind, close-hauled for sailing as close to the wind as possible. (*OED* has 'hold wind' as meaning 'keep near the wind, without making leeway')

48-49 **set her…again**: put on sail – foresail and mainsail. The previous order is immediately countermanded as they must nearly have been driven onto the shore and there is no room in which to remain close-hauled and as nearly stationary as the storm will permit and they must try to go out to sea again

• *What do Antonio's words (from line 42 to line 56) lead us to think about his character?*

to silence, and work the peace of the present, we
will not hand a rope more. Use your authority. If
you cannot, give thanks you have lived so long, and
make yourself ready in your cabin for the mischance
of the hour, if it so hap. Cheerly good hearts!   25
Out of our way I say.   [*Exit*

GONZALO   I have great comfort from this fellow. Methinks he
hath no drowning mark upon him, his complexion
is perfect gallows. Stand fast, good Fate, to his
hanging; make the rope of his destiny our cable,   30
for our own doth little advantage. If he be not born
to be hanged, our case is miserable.   [*Exeunt*

Enter BOATSWAIN

BOATSWAIN   Down with the topmast. Yare, lower; lower.
Bring her to try with main-course. [*A cry within.*] A
plague upon this howling! They are louder than   35
the weather or our office.

Enter SEBASTIAN, ANTONIO, *and* GONZALO

Yet again? What do you here? Shall we give o'er and
drown? Have you a mind to sink?

SEBASTIAN   A pox o' your throat, you bawling, blasphemous,
incharitable dog!   40

BOATSWAIN   Work you then.

ANTONIO   Hang, cur, hang, you whoreson, insolent
noisemaker. We are less afraid to be drowned than
thou art.

GONZALO   I'll warrant him for drowning, though the ship   45
were no stronger than a nutshell, and as leaky as an
unstanched wench.

BOATSWAIN   Lay her a-hold, a-hold; set her two courses off
to sea again; lay her off.

Enter MARINERS *wet*

MARINERS   All lost, to prayers, to prayers! All lost!   50

The crew and passengers see that their death is imminent. The ship is heard to split apart and Gonzalo says goodbye to the wife and children he has left at home, wishing he could be allowed to die on dry land.

51 must our...cold?: must we die? Some suggest 'cold with drink' as sailors were alleged to take to drink when nothing more practical remained to be done. Line 54 seems to back this possibility

54 merely: utterly, completely

55 wide-chapped: wide-mouthed – liable to eat and drink greedily

56 The washing of ten tides: pirates were condemned to be hanged on the shore at low tide and left during three high tides. This exaggerates the idea

57-58 Though every...glut him: Gonzalo still insists that the boatswain will not drown, however many drops of water indicate the contrary and however much it looks as though the sea will swamp him

64 long heath, broom, furze: long heath is a type of heath plant. Some editions have 'brown furze' but furze (gorse) is green unless burnt and is often seen with broom. In the exchange of sea for useless land, Gonzalo makes clear his fear of drowning.

65-66 I would fain: I would be content

On the island Prospero and Miranda are outside his 'cell'. She, used to his magic arts, suspects that he has caused the storm. She is very distressed at the suffering she has seen.

1 art: Prospero's magic powers

2 allay them: calm them down

4 welkins's cheek: the curvature of the sky

BOATSWAIN   What, must our mouths be cold?

GONZALO   The King and Prince at prayers, let's assist them, for
our case is as theirs.

SEBASTIAN   I'm out of patience.

ANTONIO   We are merely cheated of our lives by drunkards.
This wide-chapped rascal – would thou mightst lie
drowning   55
The washing of ten tides.

GONZALO   He'll be hanged yet,
Though every drop of water swear against it.
And gape at wid'st to glut him.
[*A confused noise within.*
Mercy on us! –
We split, we split – Farewell my wife and children –
Farewell brother – We split, we split, we split.   60

ANTONIO   Let's all sink wi' th' King.

SEBASTIAN   Let's take leave of him.
[*Exeunt* ANTONIO *and* SEBASTIAN

GONZALO   Now would I give a thousand furlongs of sea for an
acre of barren ground, long heath, broom, furze,
any thing. The wills above be done, but I would   65
fain die a dry death.
[*Exeunt*

Scene 2 ━━━━━━━━━

The island. Before PROSPERO's *cell*

Enter PROSPERO *and* MIRANDA

MIRANDA   If by your art, my dearest father, you have
Put the wild waters in this roar, allay them.
The sky, it seems, would pour down stinking pitch,
But that the sea, mounting to the welkin's cheek,
Dashes the fire out. O I have suffered   5
With those that I saw suffer. A brave vessel,

Miranda had admired the ship and now mourns the men who died. She insists that if she had had the power, this would not have happened. Prospero says it was all done in her best interests and no one has been harmed. He prepares to tell her something of their past.

7 **noble creature**: Miranda must have absorbed any concept of 'noble' from her father, Prospero, and in theory she has no memory of a 'brave vessel', except possibly from books

10 **I**: presumably with stress on 'I' since she sees Prospero as having this power

13 **fraughting souls**: passengers – human freight

14 **amazement**: bewilderment, confusion
piteous: full of pity

19 **more better**: a double comparative with a reinforcing effect, as Shakespeare's double negatives have

20 **full**: very, exceedingly

21 **no greater**: no more elevated in position than his 'house' suggests

22 **meddle**: mingle (possibly here with just a suggestion of the then developing meaning of 'interfere')

23–24 **Lend...me**: help me take off my magic robe. By taking it off Prospero wants to make it clear to Miranda that he is telling her a true story, as her father, without supernatural powers

25 **Lie there, my art**: he is putting aside magic for the moment

26 **direful**: dreadful, terrible

27 **virtue**: essence

28 **provision**: foresight

30 **perdition**: loss (like the modern French 'perdre' – to lose)

31 **Betid**: happened

Who had no doubt some noble creature in her,
Dashed all to pieces. O the cry did knock
Against my very heart. Poor souls, they perished.
Had I been any god of power, I would   10
Have sunk the sea within the earth, or ere
It should the good ship so have swallowed, and
The fraughting souls within her.

PROSPERO   Be collected;
No more amazement. Tell your piteous heart
There's no harm done.

MIRANDA   O woe the day!

PROSPERO   No
harm.   15
I have done nothing but in care of thee,
Of thee my dear one, thee my daughter, who
Art ignorant of what thou art, nought knowing
Of whence I am, nor that I am more better
Than Prospero, master of a full poor cell,   20
And thy no greater father.

MIRANDA   More to know
Did never meddle with my thoughts.

PROSPERO   'Tis time
I should inform thee further. Lend thy hand,
And pluck my magic garment from me. So.
                              [*Lays down his mantle*
Lie there, my art. Wipe thou thine eyes, have
    comfort.   25
The direful spectacle of the wreck, which touched
The very virtue of compassion in thee,
I have with such provision in mine art
So safely ordered, that there is no soul –
No, not so much perdition as an hair   30
Betid to any creature in the vessel
Which thou heard'st cry, which thou saw'st sink. Sit
    down,
For thou must now know further.

Prospero has decided that the moment has come to tell Miranda about their past. She was only three and can just remember her serving women, nothing more. She cannot remember coming to the island and did not know that twelve years previously her father was Duke of Milan.

35 bootless inquisition: useless questioning

40–41 not Out three years old: not more than three years old

42 By what?: What triggers this memory?

50 dark backward and abysm: Miranda has to look back to try to remember, but the past may seem like a dark chasm or abyss

56 piece of virtue: the very example of chastity

59 no worse issued: because you are their child, you are a princess

MIRANDA   You have often
Begun to tell me what I am, but stopped,
And left me to a bootless inquisition,   35
Concluding, 'Stay, not yet'.

PROSPERO   The hour's now come,
The very minute bids thee ope thine ear.
Obey, and be attentive. Canst thou remember
A time before we came unto this cell?
I do not think thou canst, for then thou wast
        not   40
Out three years old.

MIRANDA   Certainly sir, I can.

PROSPERO By what? By any other house or person?
Of any thing the image, tell me, that
Hath kept with thy remembrance.

MIRANDA   'Tis far off,
And rather like a dream than an assurance   45
That my remembrance warrants. Had I not
Four or five women once that tended me?

PROSPERO Thou hadst, and more Miranda. But how is it
That this lives in thy mind? What seest thou else
In the dark backward and abysm of time?   50
If thou remembrest aught ere thou cam'st here,
How thou cam'st here thou mayst.

MIRANDA   But that I do
        not.

PROSPERO Twelve year since, Miranda, twelve year since,
Thy father was the Duke of Milan and
A prince of power.

MIRANDA   Sir, are not you my father?   55

PROSPERO Thy mother was a piece of virtue, and
She said thou wast my daughter; and thy father
Was Duke of Milan; and his only heir,
And princess, no worse issued.

MIRANDA   O the heavens,

Prospero reveals to Miranda that he had left the affairs of state to his brother Antonio, while he immersed himself in study. His treacherous brother then started granting favours to and promoting men who would be useful to him, until, little by little, he came to be regarded as head of state.

63 holp: helped; a shortening of 'holpen' the old past participle of 'to help'

64 teen: trouble

65 is from my remembrance: I do not remember
Please you further: please go on

67–68 that a brother...perfidious: that of all people a brother should be capable of such treachery

71 signories: states of northern Italy under the rule of princes
first: most important

72–73 reputed In dignity: with a most honourable reputation

76–77 transported And rapt in: caught up in and carried along by

79–87 Being once...out on 't: Once he had perfected the art of granting requests or tactfully refusing them, of knowing who should be allowed to climb and who should be checked for trying to climb too far too fast, he either re-fashioned men I had promoted, or deflected their loyalties or changed their allegiance quite radically. When he had the key both to the officers of state and to the office itself he was able to make all the decisions. By then he was a parasite, and like the parasitic ivy on a strong tree trunk he completely sapped my power

> • *What has Prospero learnt, with hindsight, about the way a ruler needs to behave?*

	What foul play had we, that we came from
	thence? 60
	Or blessed was't we did?
PROSPERO	Both, both my girl.
	By foul play, as thou say'st, were we heaved thence,
	But blessedly holp hither.
MIRANDA	O my heart bleeds
	To think o' th' teen that I have turned you to,
	Which is from my remembrance. Please you
	further. 65
PROSPERO	My brother and thy uncle, called Antonio –
	I pray thee mark me, that a brother should
	Be so perfidious – he whom next thyself
	Of all the world I loved, and to him put
	The manage of my state; as at that time 70
	Through all the signories it was the first,
	And Prospero the prime duke, being so reputed
	In dignity, and for the liberal arts
	Without a parallel; those being all my study,
	The government I cast upon my brother, 75
	And to my state grew stranger, being transported
	And rapt in secret studies. Thy false uncle –
	Dost thou attend me?
MIRANDA	Sir, most heedfully.
PROSPERO	Being once perfected how to grant suits,
	How to deny them, who t' advance, and who 80
	To trash for over-topping, new created
	The creatures that were mine, I say, or changed
	'em,
	Or else new formed 'em; having both the key
	Of officer and office, set all hearts i' th' state
	To what tune pleased his ear; that now he was 85
	The ivy which had hid my princely trunk,
	And sucked my verdure out on 't. Thou attend'st
	not.
MIRANDA	O good sir, I do.

Prospero explains how, as he spent his time shut up with his books, his brother took advantage of the situation. Soon Antonio seemed to believe he really was the Duke of Milan and set about arranging for this to be so in fact, as well as in his mind. To achieve this he conspired with the King of Naples.

89–97 I thus...sans bound: devoting myself to private studies and the improvement of my mind, I neglected public affairs, concentrating on matters which were entirely removed from what my subjects could understand or consider useful. All this caused the bad side of my brother's nature to become dominant. My boundless confidence in him triggered as great a dishonesty on his part, just as a parent's complete trust in his son can sometimes give rise to that son's deceit

97 sans: without

lorded: made up to be a lord

98 revenue: (stress on 2nd syllable)

97–105 He...prerogative: he, having been made a lord not only with what I owned but also with the potential of my authority, like a man who in telling lies to himself makes his own memory sin by believing his lies to be true, he came to believe he really was the duke; because he had been my substitute and had carried out the public functions of royalty with all its rights and privileges

107–109 To have...Milan: to do away with the barrier between the role he acted and the man for whom he acted, he had to become fully the Duke of Milan

110 temporal: the business of political rule, as opposed to the eternal truths Prospero was seeking in his studies

111 confederates: (a verb) conspires

112 So dry...sway: his thirst for power was so great

116 ignoble stooping: humiliating subservience. Antonio, to get the help he needed had to make the formerly proud and independent dukedom of Milan subject to the King of Naples

117 Mark...event: take note of the contract he made and what resulted from it

> • *What might Antonio's feelings have been at this time?*

PROSPERO   I pray thee mark me.
I thus neglecting wordly ends, all dedicated
To closeness and the bettering of my mind   90
With that which, but by being so retired,
O'er-prized all popular rate, in my false brother
Awaked an evil nature; and my trust,
Like a good parent, did beget of him
A falsehood in its contrary as great   95
As my trust was, which had indeed no limit,
A confidence sans bound. He being thus lorded,
Not only with what my revenue yielded,
But what my power might else exact, like one
Who having into truth, by telling of it,   100
Made such a sinner of his memory,
To credit his own lie, he did believe
He was indeed the duke; out o' th' substitution,
And executing the outward face of royalty,
With all prerogative; hence his ambition
    growing –   105
Dost thou hear?

MIRANDA   Your tale, sir, would cure
deafness.

PROSPERO   To have no screen between this part he played
And him he played it for, he needs will be
Absolute Milan. Me, poor man, my library
Was dukedom large enough: of temporal
    royalties   110
He thinks me now incapable; confederates –
So dry he was for sway – wi' th' King of Naples
To give him annual tribute, do him homage,
Subject his coronet to his crown, and bend
The dukedom yet unbowed – alas, poor
    Milan! –   115
To most ignoble stooping.

MIRANDA   O the heavens!

PROSPERO   Mark his condition, and the event, then tell me

Continuing his story, Prospero tells how, as his side of the bargain, Alonso agreed to exile him from Milan, so one night he and Miranda were seized and hurried away. Prospero thinks that they were not killed there and then because the people would not have tolerated such a thing.

118–120 I...sons: this is the second suggestion in the play (see Act 1 scene 2 line 94) that 'breeding' is not necessarily a reliable indication of character

119 but: other than

121–122 an enemy To me inveterate: a long-standing enemy

123 in lieu o': in return for

125 presently extirpate: at once get rid of

131 The ministers: the men chosen

132 thy crying self: this short phrase suddenly evokes all the horror of that night

134 hint: occasion

135 wrings my eyes to 't: forces tears from my eyes. The metaphor is that of wringing out a wet cloth

137 the which: which

138 impertinent: irrelevant. 'Pertinent' has kept the meaning 'relevant' but the negative meaning has changed

140 durst: old form of 'dared'

If this might be a brother.

MIRANDA   I should sin
To think but nobly of my grandmother:
Good wombs have borne bad sons.

PROSPERO   Now the
          condition.   120
This King of Naples being an enemy
To me inveterate, hearkens my brother's suit,
Which was, that he in lieu o' th' premises
Of homage, and I know not how much tribute,
Should presently extirpate me and mine   125
Out of the dukedom, and confer fair Milan
With all the honours on my brother. Whereon,
A treacherous army levied, one midnight
Fated to the purpose, did Antonio open
The gates of Milan, and i' th' dead of darkness,   130
The ministers for th' purpose hurried thence
Me and thy crying self.

MIRANDA   Alack, for pity!
I not rememb'ring how I cried out then,
Will cry it o'er again. It is a hint
That wrings mine eyes to 't.

PROSPERO   Hear a little
          further,   135
And then I'll bring thee to the present business
Which now's upon's; without the which this story
Were most impertinent.

MIRANDA   Wherefore did they not
That hour destroy us?

PROSPERO   Well demanded, wench;
My tale provokes that question. Dear, they
          durst not,   140
So dear the love my people bore me; nor set
A mark so bloody on the business; but
With colours fairer painted their foul ends.

Father and daughter were hustled aboard a ship and then, some miles out to sea, were lowered into a rotten and leaky boat. Gonzalo, a Neapolitan put in charge of the enterprise, took pity on them to the extent of stowing food, water, clothes and some of Prospero's books in the boat. Eventually they landed on the island.

144 **In few**: in a few words, in short

145 **some leagues**: several miles

146 **carcass of a butt**: a mere tub of a boat. 'Carcass' suggests that the ribs of the boat may have been showing through in places – as in a skeleton. This boat is not fully seaworthy. In one of the repeat patterns in this play, Stephano sails in from the wreck on a butt (cask) of wine and eventually decides he will be king of the island

148 **have quit**: although 'had' would provide the proper sequence of tenses, the use of 'have' is more immediate, as though Prospero is reliving the experience

150–151 **To the winds...loving wrong**: in the sympathetic 'sighing' of the winds (see GLOSSARY page 225 Personification) Shakespeare gives them human characteristics and starts to mark the change from his urgent story of betrayal and action by humans, to their arrival on the island by God's intervention

152 **a cherubin**: an angel

154 **Infused**: filled (three syllables are needed for the metre)

155 **decked**: covered

157 **undergoing stomach**: an underlying resolution to survive; a constant and sustaining courage

161 **noble Neapolitan**: 'noble' indicates a man who acts in accordance with his morals and his conscience; a humane man. 'Neapolitan' means 'of Naples'

162 **charity**: not in the sometimes rather cold and detached use of the word today, but a combination of love for his fellow creatures, and generosity

163 **design**: (here) scheme

165 **steaded much**: been of great use
gentleness: the combination of qualities which originally formed the concept of 'gentleman' and included compassion, thoughtfulness for others, courtesy and proper behaviour (also see Chaucer's 'verray parfit, gentil knight' in *The Canterbury Tales*)

168 **prize above**: value more than

In few, they hurried us aboard a bark,
Bore us some leagues to sea, where they
   prepared   145
A rotten carcass of a butt, not rigged,
Nor tackle, sail, nor mast; the very rats
Instinctively have quit it. There they hoist us,
To cry to the sea that roared to us, to sigh
To the winds whose pity, sighing back again,   150
Did us but loving wrong.

MIRANDA   Alack, what trouble
Was I then to you.

PROSPERO   O, a cherubin
Thou wast that did preserve me. Thou didst smile,
Infused with a fortitude from heaven,
When I have decked the sea with drops full salt, 155
Under my burden groaned; which raised in me
An undergoing stomach, to bear up
Against what should ensue.

MIRANDA   How came we ashore?

PROSPERO By Providence divine.
Some food we had, and some fresh water that   160
A noble Neapolitan, Gonzalo,
Out of his charity, who being then appointed
Master of this design, did give us, with
Rich garments, linens, stuffs, and necessaries,
Which since have steaded much; so of his
   gentleness,   165
Knowing I loved my books, he furnished me
From mine own library with volumes that
I prize above my dukedom.

MIRANDA   Would I might
But ever see that man.

PROSPERO   Now I arise.
                                [*Resumes his mantle*
Sit still, and hear the last of our sea-sorrow.   170
Here in this island we arrived, and here

Prospero tells Miranda he has taught her more than other
princesses know. When she asks his reason for raising the storm,
he says his enemies have been sent by fate to the island and he
must act now if he is to profit from his favourable star. He sends
her to sleep and calls Ariel who has come from orchestrating the
tempest and the shipwreck.

172 **made thee more profit**: caused you to be better educated than
    other princesses who have more spare time for amusements
176 **beating**: thrashing around
178 **bountiful**: generous
179 **Now**: at present. This points up the traditionally changeable,
    fickle nature of Fortune, personified frequently, as here, as a
    lady
180 **prescience**: foreknowledge, knowledge of events before they
    happen
180–184 **And by my prescience...droop**: Prospero, through his
    knowledge of magic and astrology is aware of a favourable star
    – but if he fails to grasp this opportunity for good fortune, his
    prospects will only decline
181 **zenith**: highest point, peak (of a career for instance)
185 **'Tis a good dulness**: there is nothing wrong with this
    drowsiness
186 **give it way**: you can give way to it
    I know...choose: it has been induced by Prospero's magic art
187 **Come away**: come here
190 **To answer...pleasure**: to carry out anything you may ask me to
    do
192 **task**: (a verb) 'give a task to'
193 **quality**: the lesser spirits Ariel has at his command
194 **to point**: exactly
196 **beak**: prow
197 **waist**: amidships
    deck: the poop deck, a raised deck in the stern of the ship
198 **I flamed amazement**: my appearance as flames brought terror
200 **yards**: spars slung from a mast to support a square sail
    distinctly: in several different places. Before and after a storm at
    sea, flames were sometimes seen to play over ships. They were
    called 'St. Elmo's fire' after the Spanish patron saint of sailors
201 **Jove**: the chief of the gods, in charge of thunder and lightning

	Have I, thy schoolmaster, made thee more profit	
	Than other princesses can, that have more time	
	For vainer hours, and tutors not so careful.	

MIRANDA   Heavens thank you for 't. And now I pray you sir,   175
For still 'tis beating in my mind, your reason
For raising this sea-storm?

PROSPERO   Know thus far forth.
By accident most strange, bountiful Fortune,
Now my dear lady, hath mine enemies
Brought to this shore. And by my prescience   180
I find my zenith doth depend upon
A most auspicious star, whose influence
If now I court not, but omit, my fortunes
Will ever after droop. Here cease more questions;
Thou art inclined to sleep. 'Tis a good dulness,   185
And give it way. I know thou canst not choose.
                              [MIRANDA *sleeps*
Come away, servant, come. I am ready now.
Approach my Ariel, come.

Enter ARIEL

ARIEL   All hail, great master! Grave sir, hail! I come
To answer thy best pleasure; be 't to fly,   190
To swim, to dive into the fire, to ride
On the curled clouds; to thy strong bidding task
Ariel, and all his quality.

PROSPERO   Hast thou, spirit,
Performed to point the tempest that I bade thee?

ARIEL   To every article.   195
I boarded the King's ship; now on the beak,
Now in the waist, the deck, in every cabin,
I flamed amazement. Sometime I'd divide,
And burn in many places; on the topmast,
The yards and bowsprit, would I flame distinctly,   200
Then meet and join. Jove's lightnings, the

Ariel describes, in loving detail, the storm he helped Prospero to raise. It was enough to drive all on board mad and all except the sailors dived into the sea. Ferdinand was the first to jump. He is on his own somewhere on the island. Neither he nor the rest of the royal party has suffered any injury.

202–203 more momentary And sight-outrunning: swift and sudden

204 sulphurous roaring: lightning (sulphur burns with a bluish flame and the smell of rotten eggs)

Neptune: the Roman god of the sea, often shown with a trident, a three-pronged spear

207 Who was...?: can anyone have been...?

coil: disturbance, row, uproar

208 infect his reason?: drive him mad?

209 a fever of the mad: confusion such as madmen feel

210 All but mariners: everyone except the seamen

212 all afire with me: apparently in flames as the result of my work

213 hair up-staring: hair standing on end

216 nigh: near

218 sustaining garments: there is discussion about whether their clothes would have dragged them down, or supported them long enough to get them to the shore, but in any case Prospero's questioning has moved to the present tense 'are they safe?' and their garments certainly sustain them now, on shore: in comfort, in dignity and in rank

223 angle: corner

224 His arms in this sad knot: his arms folded dejectedly, like this

225 thou hast disposed: you have dealt with

- *How does Prospero show his concern for the safety of the ship-wreck victims? Why is he so concerned?*

precursors
O' th' dreadful thunder-claps, more momentary
And sight-outrunning were not; the fire and cracks
Of sulphurous roaring the most mighty Neptune
Seem to besiege, and make his bold waves
     tremble,   205
Yea, his dread trident shake.

PROSPERO   My brave spirit,
Who was so firm, so constant, that this coil
Would not infect his reason?

ARIEL   Not a soul
But felt a fever of the mad, and played
Some tricks of desperation. All but mariners   210
Plunged in the foaming brine, and quit the vessel,
Then all afire with me. The King's son Ferdinand,
With hair up-staring – then like reeds, not hair –
Was the first man that leaped; cried, 'Hell is empty,
And all the devils are here'.

PROSPERO   Why, that's my
     spirit.   215
But was not this nigh shore?

                                 Close by, my master.

PROSPERO   But are they, Ariel, safe?

ARIEL   Not a hair perished;
On their sustaining garments not a blemish,
But fresher than before. And, as thou bad'st me,
In troops I have dispersed them 'bout the isle.   220
The King's son have I landed by himself,
Whom I left cooling of the air with sighs
In an odd angle of the isle, and sitting,
His arms in this sad knot.

PROSPERO   Of the King's ship,
The mariners, say how thou hast disposed,   225
And all the rest o' th' fleet.

ARIEL   Safely in harbour

Ariel continues his account of the shipwreck. The king's ship, with the sailors under hatches, is safe in an inlet and the other vessels in the fleet have turned back for Naples. Asked to do some more work, Ariel starts to remind Prospero about the freedom he had previously promised him.

229 **Bermoothes**: the Bermudas (see page 211)
231 **suffered labour**: the hard work they had suffered in the storm
234 **flote**: flood, meaning 'sea'
239 **mid season**: midday
240 **two glasses**: two hour-glasses – two o'clock
242 **pains**: tasks, labours
243 **remember**: remind
244 **Moody?...demand?**: the atmosphere of congratulation swiftly changes when Ariel reminds Prospero of his promises. Prospero has to remain in control if his plans are to work
250 **bate**: abate, shorten my service, let me off

> • *Notice how long the action of the play will take.*

Is the King's ship; in the deep nook, where once
Thou call'dst me up at midnight to fetch dew
From the still-vexed Bermoothes, there she's hid;
The mariners all under hatches stowed,   230
Who, with a charm joined to their suffered labour,
I have left asleep. And for the rest o' th' fleet,
Which I dispersed, they all have met again,
And are upon the Mediterranean flote,
Bound sadly home for Naples,   235
Supposing that they saw the King's ship wrecked,
And his great person perish.

PROSPERO   Ariel, thy charge
Exactly is performed. But there's more work.
What is the time o' th' day?

ARIEL   Past the mid season.

PROSPERO   At least two glasses. The time 'twixt six and
           now   240
Must by us both be spent most preciously.

ARIEL   Is there more toil? Since thou dost give me pains,
Let me remember thee what thou hast promised,
Which is not yet performed me.

PROSPERO   How now?
           Moody?
What is 't thou canst demand?

ARIEL   My liberty.   245

PROSPERO   Before the time be out? No more.

ARIEL   I prithee,
Remember I have done thee worthy service,
Told thee no lies, made no mistakings, served
Without or grudge or grumblings; thou didst
           promise
To bate me a full year.

PROSPERO   Dost thou forget   250
From what a torment I did free thee?

ARIEL   No.

Prospero has to remind Ariel of the torment he had to endure when the witch Sycorax had him in her power. Because he had refused to obey her grosser commands, she had imprisoned him in a pine tree. He had been there for twelve years until released through Prospero's magic powers.

252 ooze: mud, silt

253 deep: ocean

256 baked: hardened, caked

257 malignant thing: compare later epithets for Caliban

258 Sycorax: the name does not appear anywhere else. It may be a combination of the Greek words for 'pig' and 'raven'. Similarities have also been suggested with the witch Circe who, in Greek myth changed Odysseus' men into pigs, and seduced him into spending a year with her

259 Was grown into a hoop: a vivid description of the old witch, bent almost round

261 Argier: an old name for Algiers

O, was she so?: this is either Prospero's sarcastic reaction, suggesting his irritation at having constantly to remind Ariel of his misery under Sycorax, or, just possibly, a reaction on stage to an unexpected contemporary reference (see INTRODUCTION page xiii Background)

266–267 for...life: Sycorax's life was spared in much the same way as Prospero's and Miranda's. She had either done one good deed to 'earn' this, or her life was spared because she was pregnant

269 blue-eyed hag: with dark circles round her eyes, or with blue eyelids, taken to be an indication of pregnancy

273 earthy and abhorred: gross and detestable

274 hests: commands

275 potent ministers: powerful spirits

276 unmitigable: that could not be made less

277 cloven: split, the trunk had been split and, then, with Ariel inside, fixed back together again

281 mill-wheels strike: the slapping sound made by the blades of a water-wheel when they hit the water

282 litter: normally used of animals

PROSPERO	Thou dost, and think'st it much to tread the ooze
	Of the salt deep,
	To run upon the sharp wind of the north,
	To do me business in the veins o' th' earth 255
	When it is baked with frost.
ARIEL	I do not sir.
PROSPERO	Thou liest, malignant thing. Hast thou forgot
	The foul witch Sycorax, who with age and envy
	Was grown into a hoop? Hast thou forgot her?
ARIEL	No sir.
PROSPERO	Thou hast. Where was she born? Speak;
	tell me. 260
ARIEL	Sir, in Argier.
PROSPERO	O, was she so? I must
	Once in a month recount what thou hast been,
	Which thou forget'st. This damned witch Sycorax,
	For mischiefs manifold, and sorceries terrible
	To enter human hearing, from Argier, 265
	Thou know'st was banished: for one thing she did
	They would not take her life. Is not this true?
ARIEL	Ay sir.
PROSPERO	This blue-eyed hag was hither brought with child,
	And here was left by the sailors. Thou my slave, 270
	As thou report'st thyself, wast then her servant;
	And for thou wast a spirit too delicate
	To act her earthy and abhorred commands,
	Refusing her grand hests, she did confine thee
	By help of her more potent ministers, 275
	And in her most unmitigable rage,
	Into a cloven pine; within which rift
	Imprisoned thou didst painfully remain
	A dozen years; within which space she died,
	And left thee there; where thou didst vent thy
	groans 280
	As fast as mill-wheels strike. Then was this island –
	Save for the son that she did litter here,

Sycorax, having been exiled when she was pregnant, gave birth
to Caliban on the island. He is now Prospero's servant. Ariel
had been condemned to live in agony in the pine trunk.
Prospero, by his skill, was able to free him, but he now
threatens him with similar imprisonment in an oak tree if he
complains again. Otherwise, he will free Ariel from his service
in two days' time. He orders Ariel to become an invisible sea-
nymph.

283 **whelp**: the young of wild animals or of any creature regarded
with dislike or distaste
285 **Dull thing, I say so**: Prospero resents the interruption: it is
his story
294 **If...murmur'st**: if you grumble any more
294–295 **I will...entrails**: Prospero threatens him with a similar
fate to the one he suffered under Sycorax – only the tree is
different
297 **correspondent**: obedient
298 **spriting**: duties as a sprite
301 **nymph o' the sea**: in Greek myth nymphs were the
personification of various natural objects: rivers, trees,
mountains and lakes. There were fifty sea-nymphs, often
called Nereids, who were daughters of a sea-god, Nereus

- *How does Shakespeare give all of the information
  which the audience needs to know?*
- *What methods does Prospero use to control Ariel?*

A freckled whelp hag-born – not honoured with
A human shape.

ARIEL   Yes, Caliban her son.

PROSPERO   Dull thing, I say so; he, that Caliban   285
Whom now I keep in service. Thou best know'st
What torment I did find thee in; thy groans
Did make wolves howl, and penetrate the breasts
Of ever-angry bears. It was a torment
To lay upon the damned, which Sycorax   290
Could not again undo. It was mine art,
When I arrived and heard thee, that made gape
The pine, and let thee out.

ARIEL   I thank thee master.

PROSPERO   If thou more murmur'st, I will rend an oak,
And peg thee in his knotty entrails, till   295
Thou hast howled away twelve winters.

ARIEL   Pardon,
           master,
I will be correspondent to command,
And do my spriting gently.

PROSPERO   Do so, and after two
           days
I will discharge thee.

ARIEL   That's my noble master.
What shall I do? Say what. What shall I do?   300

PROSPERO   Go make thyself like a nymph o' the sea. Be subject
To no sight but thine and mine, invisible
To every eyeball else. Go take this shape
And hither come in 't. Go. Hence with diligence.
                                        [*Exit* ARIEL
Awake, dear heart awake, thou hast slept well;   305
Awake.

MIRANDA   The strangeness of your story put
Heaviness in me.

PROSPERO   Shake it off. Come on,

Once Miranda is awake, she and Prospero go to visit Caliban,
their slave. The dislike, even hatred, on either side is obvious.
Caliban's reluctance to obey brings threats from Prospero.

311 **miss**: do without
312 **serves in offices**: does duties
314 **earth**: Caliban is of the earth, Ariel a spirit of the air
316 **when?**: with all the irritation of 'when are you going to come
out?' and 'how much longer must I wait?'
317 **quaint**: a combination of skilful, clever, ingenious and
handsome
319 **got by**: fathered by
321–322 **As wicked...fen**: again a reference to collecting
ingredients for spells (fenland seems to have an unwholesome
image – in *Macbeth* the witches use 'fillet of a fenny snake') or
a reference to Sycorax, part raven, feeding on dew
323 **A south west**: a southwest wind, often damp and apparently
encouraging disease and disability
326 **pen thy breath up**: make you catch your breath
urchins: hedgehogs or goblins, or goblins having taken the
shape of hedgehogs; either or both would come out at night
327 **for that vast of night**: throughout a night that seems endless
329 **As thick as honeycomb**: the pinches will be as close together
as the cells in a honeycomb

	We'll visit Caliban my slave, who never Yields us kind answer.	
MIRANDA	'Tis a villain, sir, I do not love to look on.	
PROSPERO	But as 'tis, We cannot miss him. He does make our fire, Fetch in our wood, and serves in offices That profit us. What ho! Slave! Caliban! Thou earth, thou! Speak.	310
CALIBAN	[*Within*] There's wood enough within.	
PROSPERO	Come forth, I say, there's other business for thee. Come thou tortoise, when?	315

Enter ARIEL *like a water-nymph*

	Fine apparition. My quaint Ariel, Hark in thine ear.	
ARIEL	My lord, it shall be done. [*Exit*	
PROSPERO	Thou poisonous slave, got by the devil himself Upon thy wicked dam, come forth.	320

Enter CALIBAN

CALIBAN	As wicked dew as e'er my mother brushed With raven's feather from unwholesome fen Drop on you both. A south-west blow on ye, And blister you all o'er.	
PROSPERO	For this, be sure, tonight thou shalt have cramps, Side-stitches that shall pen thy breath up; urchins Shall, for that vast of night that they may work, All exercise on thee; thou shalt be pinched As thick as honeycomb, each pinch more stinging Than bees that made 'em.	325
CALIBAN	I must eat my dinner.	330

Caliban launches into an account of his relationship with Prospero. At first, as Prospero's pupil, Caliban loved him and taught him in return what he knew about the island. However, after he had tried to rape Miranda, Caliban was treated as a slave and a prisoner and now there is only resentment and hatred on both sides.

334–335 how To name...less: the name of the sun and the moon
338 The fresh...fertile: Caliban generously showed the newcomers everything that he had had to learn by trial and error
342 sty me: shut me up like a beast in a sty
345 stripes: beatings
347–348 violate The honour: rape
351 Abhorred: detested
352 Which...not take: the suggestion is that Caliban, because of what he is, is incapable of any improvement
357–358 I endowed...them known: I gave words to your intentions that enabled you to understand them

> • *Caliban on the one side and Prospero and Miranda on the other are now in opposition. Has each side good reason to loathe the other? Which side has been more mistreated?*

This island's mine, by Sycorax my mother,
Which thou tak'st from me. When thou cam'st first
Thou strok'st me and made much of me; wouldst
    give me
Water with berries in 't; and teach me how
To name the bigger light, and how the less,   335
That burn by day and night. And then I loved thee,
And showed thee all the qualities o' th' isle,
The fresh springs, brine-pits, barren place and
    fertile;
Cursed be I that did so. All the charms
Of Sycorax, toads, beetles, bats, light on you.   340
For I am all the subjects that you have,
Which first was mine own king. And here you sty
    me
In this hard rock, whiles you do keep from me
The rest o' th' island.

PROSPERO   Thou most lying slave,
Whom stripes may move, not kindness! I have used
    thee,   345
Filth as thou art, with human care, and lodged thee
In mine own cell, till thou didst seek to violate
The honour of my child.

CALIBAN   O ho, O ho, would't had been done!
Thou didst prevent me; I had peopled else   350
This isle with Calibans.

MIRANDA   Abhorred slave,
Which any print of goodness wilt not take,
Being capable of all ill, I pitied thee,
Took pains to make thee speak, taught thee each
    hour
One thing or other. When thou didst not,
    savage,   355
Know thine own meaning, but wouldst gabble like
A thing most brutish, I endowed thy purposes
With words that made them known. But thy vile
    race,

Prospero insists that Caliban do what he is ordered or be punished.
All Caliban can do is curse in the language he has been taught, and
obey. As he leaves, Ariel enters, invisible to all but Prospero (and
the audience) singing, followed by Ferdinand.

363 **my profit on 't**: what I have gained from it
364 **The red plague**: the description of one kind of plague with
    skin eruptions and sores
366–367 **be quick...other business**: you'd better be quick about it,
    there's plenty more work for you to do
369 **old cramps**: cramps such as he has been tormented with before
373 **my dam's god, Setebos**: a god of the Patagonians. The
    Patagonians were South American Indians living in a coastal
    area of the Argentine. Setebos was mentioned in accounts of
    Magellan's voyages. Magellan (*c.*1480–1521), a Portuguese
    explorer, having set out to circumnavigate the globe in 1519,
    sailed along the coast of Patagonia
377 **Courtsied...kissed**: the prelude to many country dances
    The wild waves whist: there is much discussion about the
    syntax (grammar) of this part of the sentence, and therefore its
    meaning. Since it is essentially Ariel's presence and Ariel's music
    which have calmed the storm, 'the waves fall silent' seems the
    most satisfactory explanation
379 **featly**: neatly and gracefully
380 **burden**: either the 'undersong', an ongoing accompaniment
    (usually of a repeated word or words) or, more likely here, in
    view of what follows, a chorus or refrain
381–385 **Bow-wow...Cock-a-diddle-dow**: possibly just animal
    and bird noises forming the refrain. On the other hand, both
    sounds can indicate the coming of dawn, when traditionally
    spirits must return to their own world

Though thou didst learn, had that in 't which good
  natures
Could not abide to be with; therefore wast
  thou   360
Deservedly confined into this rock,
Who hadst deserved more than a prison.

CALIBAN   You taught me language, and my profit on 't
Is, I know how to curse. The red plague rid you
For learning me your language.

PROSPERO   Hag-seed,
  hence!   365
Fetch us in fuel, and be quick, thou 'rt best,
To answer other business. Shrug'st thou, malice?
If thou neglect'st, or dost unwillingly
What I command, I'll rack thee with old cramps,
Fill all thy bones with aches, make thee roar,   370
That beasts shall tremble at thy din.

CALIBAN   No, pray thee.
[*Aside*] I must obey, his art is of such power,
It would control my dam's god Setebos,
And make a vassal of him.

PROSPERO   So slave, hence.
                           [*Exit* CALIBAN

Enter ARIEL, *invisible, playing and singing;*
FERDINAND *following*

[ARIEL'S *song*]
  Come unto these yellow sands,   375
    And then take hands.
  Courtsied when you have and kissed
    The wild waves whist.
  Foot it featly here and there,
  And sweet sprites the burden bear.   380
    Hark, hark!
  Burden [*dispersedly*]   Bow-wow.
  The watch-dogs bark:

Ferdinand, sitting grieving over the loss of his father, has heard Ariel's music and been drawn to follow it. When the song changes subject to sing of his father's death, Ferdinand realises it is not human singing. Prospero and Miranda approach and Miranda is impressed at the sight of Ferdinand.

398–400 Nothing...strange: Ariel sings the truth in these lines, but with an ambiguity that hides it from Ferdinand

403 ditty: song

405 owes: owns

406–407 The fringed...yond: this very formal language for 'open your eyes' or 'look up now' marks a very important and solemn moment for Prospero as well as for Miranda. He has arranged the wreck with her future in mind. This is the moment when he will see whether his match-making will work on someone who has never seen a young man before

409 a brave form: a splendid shape

411 gallant: fine gentleman

412 and but: and except for the fact that
stained: immediately suggests tear-stained

413 beauty's canker: a metaphor often used by Shakespeare. Canker is a disease, especially of fruit trees and roses, causing decay; there is also the canker-worm, a grub which eats into buds. Until around 1700 the word was also used for 'cancer' and anything which destroys in secret

Burden [*dispersedly*]　　Bow-wow.
Hark, hark! I hear
The strain of strutting chanticleer.
Cry, *Burden* [*dispersedly*] Cock-a-diddle-dow. 385

FERDINAND　　Where should this music be? I' th' air or th' earth?
It sounds no more. And sure it waits upon
Some god o' th' island. Sitting on a bank,
Weeping again the King my father's wreck,
This music crept by me upon the waters,　　　390
Allaying both their fury and my passion
With its sweet air. Thence I have followed it,
Or it hath drawn me rather. But 'tis gone.
No, it begins again.

[ARIEL *sings*]
Full fathom five thy father lies,　　　395
　　Of his bones are coral made,
Those are pearls that were his eyes;
　　Nothing of him that doth fade
But doth suffer a sea-change
Into something rich and strange.　　　400
Sea-nymphs hourly ring his knell:
　　　　　　　　　　Burden. Ding-dong.
Hark! now I hear them — Ding-dong, bell.

FERDINAND　　The ditty does remember my drowned father.
This is no mortal business, nor no sound
That the earth owes. I hear it now above me.　405

PROSPERO　　The fringed curtains of thine eye advance,
And say what thou seest yond.

MIRANDA　　　　　　　　　　What is 't! A spirit?
Lord, how it looks about. Believe me sir,
It carries a brave form. But 'tis a spirit.

PROSPERO　　No wench, it eats and sleeps, and hath such senses 410
As we have, such. This gallant which thou seest
Was in the wreck; and but he's something stained
With grief, that's beauty's canker, thou mightst call
him

Ferdinand and Miranda swiftly come to understand that they are both human and that Miranda actually speaks Ferdinand's language. Prospero rebukes Ferdinand for suggesting he is 'the best' and mentions the King of Naples. Ferdinand is convinced that all who were on the ship are now dead.

414 **goodly**: handsome

416 **natural**: naturally occurring i.e. that she has ever seen on the island

417 **It goes on...prompts it**: it progresses, my charm is working as I intend it to

418 **spirit**: addressed to Ariel

420 **On whom...attend**: whose presence is accompanied by this music

420–421 **Vouchsafe...May know**: grant my request to know whether

421 **remain**: live (compare this with modern Scottish dialect: Where do you stay? means Where are you living?)

423 **How I may...here**: conduct myself here, or, more likely, manage to keep going (survive) here
prime: most important. The whole sentence is equivalent to 'and last but not least'

424 **wonder**: a play on the name of Miranda, without Ferdinand realising it

425 **maid**: girl, young woman

428 **How?**: what do you mean?

430 **single**: solitary, alone, with a play on another meaning: poor, weak, feeble, as he is not only alone but deprived of every support he is used to

431–432 **He does...I weep**: the King of Naples does hear me and so I weep. Ferdinand thinks he is now the King of Naples, after his father's supposed death, and he is hearing his own words

433 **never since at ebb**: the tide flowing from my eyes has never since retreated

436 **his brave son**: there is no other mention of Antonio's son and he is not in the list of characters. Possibly an earlier plotting idea of Shakespeare's which he then abandoned

A goodly person. He hath lost his fellows,
And strays about to find 'em.

MIRANDA   I might call him   415
A thing divine, for nothing natural
I ever saw so noble.

PROSPERO   [*Aside*]   It goes on I see
As my soul prompts it. Spirit, fine spirit, I'll free
    thee
Within two days for this.

FERDINAND   Most sure, the
    goddess
On whom these airs attend. Vouchsafe my   420
    prayer
May know if you remain upon this island,
And that you will some good instruction give
How I may bear me here. My prime request,
Which I do last pronounce, is – O you
    wonder –
If you be maid or no?

MIRANDA   No wonder sir,   425
But certainly a maid.

FERDINAND   My language? Heavens,
I am the best of them that speak this speech,
Were I but where 'tis spoken.

PROSPERO   How? The best?
What wert thou if the King of Naples heard
    thee?

FERDINAND   A single thing, as I am now, that wonders   430
To hear thee speak of Naples. He does hear me,
And that he does I weep. Myself am Naples,
Who with mine eyes, never since at ebb, beheld
The King my father wrecked.

MIRANDA   Alack, for mercy!

FERDINAND   Yes faith, and all his lords, the Duke of Milan   435
And his brave son being twain.

Prospero sees that Miranda and Ferdinand have fallen in love at first sight, but now fears that this relationship will have less value in their eyes, because it has all been so easy. Accordingly he appears to become unpleasant, pretending that Ferdinand is a spy, looking to take the island from him.

437 **more braver**: another double comparative for emphasis
     control: prove you wrong
438 **If now 'twere fit**: if now were the right time
439 **changed eyes**: fallen in love at first sight
     delicate: ingenious
441 **done yourself some wrong**: made a mistake
445 **if a virgin**: Ferdinand returns to his question in line 424
449 **lest...light**: in case the ease with which they become engaged makes the prize seem trivial
451–452 **Thou dost...ow'st not**: you are taking for yourself a name you do not own
455 **temple**: essentially the dwelling-place of a deity. When the human body is perceived as a temple it is seen as something sacred, the place inhabited by the precious spirit of the person
461 **fresh-brook mussels**: not considered good to eat

> • *Why does Prospero keep repeating 'I'll set thee free for this'?*
> • *Why does the audience need to understand Prospero's scheme in order for the scene to work?*

PROSPERO	[*Aside*] The Duke of Milan
	And his more braver daughter could control thee,
	If now 'twere fit to do 't. At the first sight
	They have changed eyes. Delicate Ariel,
	I'll set thee free for this. A word good sir, 440
	I fear you have done yourself some wrong. A word.
MIRANDA	Why speaks my father so ungently? This
	Is the third man that e'er I saw, the first
	That e'er I sighed for. Pity move my father
	To be inclined my way.
FERDINAND	O, if a virgin, 445
	And your affection not gone forth, I'll make you
	The Queen of Naples.
PROSPERO	Soft sir, one word more.
	[*Aside*] They are both in either's powers. But this
	swift business
	I must uneasy make, lest too light winning
	Make the prize light. One word more. I charge
	thee 450
	That thou attend me. Thou dost here usurp
	The name thou ow'st not, and hast put thyself
	Upon this island as a spy, to win it
	From me, the lord on 't.
FERDINAND	No, as I am a man.
MIRANDA	There's nothing ill can dwell in such a temple: 455
	If the ill spirit have so fair a house,
	Good things will strive to dwell with 't.
PROSPERO	Follow
	me.
	Speak not you for him. He's a traitor. Come,
	I'll manacle thy neck and feet together.
	Sea-water shalt thou drink. Thy food shall be 460
	The fresh-brook mussels, withered roots, and husks
	Wherein the acorn cradled. Follow.
FERDINAND	No,
	I will resist such entertainment till

Ferdinand draws his sword, but cannot use it, because
Prospero puts a spell on him. Although Miranda protests at
Prospero's apparent cruelty, he insists that Ferdinand go with
him and even threatens her with his anger.

465 **rash**: hasty
466 **not fearful**: not frightening, not threatening
467 **My foot my tutor?**: I'm supposed to let my foot rule my
      head now, am I?
469 **Come from thy ward**: give up that defensive position
      (position taken up prior to a bout of swordplay)
470 **this stick**: Prospero's magician's staff
473 **surety**: guarantee
474 **chide**: scold, rebuke
482 **Thy nerves...again**: your sinews are like those of a new-born
      baby
483 **vigour**: strength
486 **nor**: 'and' rather than 'nor' makes more sense here. It may be
      a confusion of two possible constructions

Mine enemy has more power.
　　　　　　[*Draws, and is charmed from moving*

MIRANDA 　　　　　　　　　　　O dear father,
Make not too rash a trial of him, for　　　　465
He's gentle, and not fearful.

PROSPERO 　　　　　　　　　　What, I say?
My foot my tutor? Put thy sword up traitor;
Who makest a show, but darest not strike; thy
　　　conscience
Is so possessed with guilt. Come from thy
　　　ward,
For I can here disarm thee with this stick,　　470
And make thy weapon drop.

MIRANDA 　　　　　　　　　　Beseech you, father.

PROSPERO   Hence! Hang not on my garments.

MIRANDA 　　　　　　　　　　　Sir have pity.
I'll be his surety.

PROSPERO 　　　　　　Silence. One word more
Shall make me chide thee, if not hate thee.
　　　What,
An advocate for an impostor? Hush.　　　475
Thou think'st there is no more such shapes as he,
Having seen but him and Caliban. Foolish wench,
To the most of men this is a Caliban.
And they to him are angels.

MIRANDA 　　　　　　　　　　My affections
Are then most humble; I have no ambition　　480
To see a goodlier man.

PROSPERO 　　　　　　　　Come on, obey.
Thy nerves are in their infancy again,
And have no vigour in them.

FERDINAND 　　　　　　　　　So they are.
My spirits, as in a dream, are all bound up.
My father's loss, the weakness which I feel,　　485
The wreck of all my friends, nor this man's threats,

Ferdinand is resigned to being imprisoned as long as he can see Miranda. Prospero is pleased with his scheming and with Ariel. Miranda tries to console Ferdinand.

495 **Than...by speech**: than his words may suggest
   unwonted: not typical
497–498 **but then...command**: but if this is to happen, you must carry out every detail of my orders

                    To whom I am subdued, are but light to me,
                    Might I but through my prison once a day
                    Behold this maid. All corners else o' th' earth
                    Let liberty make use of. Space enough   490
                    Have I in such a prison.

PROSPERO   *[Aside]*   It works. [*To* FERDINAND]
                    Come on.
                    [*To* ARIEL] Thou hast done well, fine Ariel!
                    [*To* FERDINAND]   Follow
                    me.
                    [*To* ARIEL] Hark what thou else shalt do me.

MIRANDA   Be
                    of comfort,
                    My father's of a better nature, sir,
                    Than he appears by speech. This is unwonted   495
                    Which now came from him.

PROSPERO   Thou shalt be as free
                    As mountain winds; but then exactly do
                    All points of my command.

ARIEL   To th' syllable.

PROSPERO   Come, follow. Speak not for him.   500
                                      [Exeunt

ACTIVITIES

Keeping track

Scene 1

1 In the storm, what is the particular danger to the ship?
2 Why do Alonso and Antonio want to speak to the ship's master?
3 What does the boatswain try to do to save the ship?
4 Why do Sebastian and Antonio speak so aggressively to the boatswain?
5 What is Gonzalo's attitude to what is going on?
6 What seems to be the fate of the ship and those on board at the end of the scene?

Scene 2

1 What is Miranda's concern at the beginning of scene 2?
2 Does Miranda find it easy to believe *'there's no harm done'*?
3 Why does Prospero take off his magician's gown?
4 How does Prospero explain his assertion that everyone on the ship is safe?
5 How old was Miranda when her father was deposed as Duke of Milan?
6 How much does she claim to remember of her previous life?
7 Why did Prospero leave so much power in his brother's hands?
8 What made Antonio conspire with the King of Naples?
9 Why did Antonio not simply have Prospero and Miranda killed?
10 How did Gonzalo, in charge of putting father and daughter into an unseaworthy boat, show his compassion?
11 Can you suggest why Gonzalo finds the idea of death by drowning so horrifying?
12 Ariel is an unwilling but obedient servant to Prospero. What makes him unwilling and what makes him obedient?
13 Caliban is even more unwilling to serve Prospero. Why is his resentment so strong?
14 Why do Prospero and Miranda use such vicious name-calling when speaking to Caliban?
15 Prospero's match-making results in Ferdinand and Miranda falling in love instantly. How does this happen?
16 What makes Prospero appear to turn against Ferdinand?

Discussion

A Scene 1 and scene 2 are so very different that they might almost have come from different plays. Start to investigate these differences by looking at the obvious points of difference, and then consider how our interest is held again in scene 2.

1 How many characters are there in each scene?
  What is happening on stage? Are the relationships complex or simple? What cross-currents of authority are there, for example, in scene 1? In scene 2 are we simply witnessing loving father speaking to dutiful daughter?
2 Shakespeare often uses prose when 'ordinary' people speak. What advantage does prose have over blank verse in a scene of violent action and very forthright speech from both sailors and nobility? Look at the length of the speeches as well as the content.

Now move on to think about how Shakespeare manages the transition from scene 1 to scene 2 and how what we learn in scene 2 illuminates scene 1.

3 What is the subject matter of Miranda's first speech? How is it expressed? How strong is the imagery?
4 How do we know that Miranda is more than an unsuspecting spectator? What does this tell us about her feelings as she watched the wreck?
5 With the hindsight provided by scene 2 can you find any indications of the supernatural element in scene 1?
6 As Prospero starts his main narrative, which detail firmly establishes the link with scene 1, and makes his audience recognise the connection and listen for more?

B Prospero is absolute ruler on the island – in many ways more powerful than he was in Milan.

7 In what ways does he 'manage' Ariel
                                      Caliban
                                      Miranda?
8 What means do Ariel and Caliban have to challenge him?
9 Why does Prospero choose this moment, after twelve years of silence, to unburden himself of the story of his and Miranda's past?
10 In his narrative is there any evidence that he also sees Antonio's side of the story?
11 Prospero's special knowledge of books and magic has given him power. Why has Caliban's special knowledge about the island not done the same for him? How has he reacted to the loss of his secrets?
12 Would you say, from what you know so far, that Prospero has used his power well, or can you find aspects to criticise?

13 Can you suggest any additional reasons (besides the one he gives) for Prospero's sudden change of direction in his treatment of Ferdinand?

C In Act 1 scene 1, we have witnessed a dramatic example of what Prospero can achieve through his magic powers and control over spirits.

14 He now has his old enemies at his mercy. What do we expect to happen to them? (Consider the vengeance he has taken on Caliban for trying to mate with Miranda.)
15 Does it seem likely that the play will end, as *Hamlet* does, with a heap of corpses? The dealings with Ferdinand may offer a clue.
16 Is the outcome going to depend merely on the whim of Prospero?
17 The wrong done to Prospero was twelve years ago. How might this affect his behaviour?

Drama

1 We have only Prospero's version of events in Milan, before his younger brother Antonio became traitor and usurper. Even so, Prospero has the grace partly to blame himself for the way he allowed matters to deteriorate. Use HOTSEATING (page 196) to find out what motivated Antonio, what he thought and felt and how he came to the extreme action of getting rid of father and daughter.
2 Much plotting and planning must have gone on before Antonio was able to persuade Alonso to join him in his schemes. Improvise a round-table discussion between Antonio and his cronies and a couple of representatives from the court of Naples. It has to be secretive, and it has to be diplomatic and avoid completely words like 'coup', 'takeover', 'exile', 'murder'. It also has to go at least part of the way to achieving the desired result. Take time to explore ways round these problems. You may find help in the newspapers, or televised political interviews – listen for phrases and tones of voice which conceal rather than reveal information or which do not altogether mean what they appear to say.
3 In groups of three read carefully the scene (Act 1 scene 2 lines 313–374) where both Prospero and Miranda verbally abuse and threaten Caliban. Select the abusive words and phrases and enough of Caliban's responses to show his attitude – you will have to cut his speeches, but make sure the words still make sense.

Within your group share out the three parts. Choose all the different possible ways of managing this part of the scene:

- Is Caliban surly and unwilling? Is he quiet and cold, or does he shout?

- Are Prospero and Miranda loud and angry, or 'superior' and distant?
- Is it a confrontation between two cultures which will never understand each other?
- Do they come close to Caliban and use threatening gestures as well as words? Does he cower away or stand up to them? Are they a little afraid of him?
- Can Caliban rouse his audience to sympathy, or will it side with the persecutors?
- Talk about all the possibilities you can read into the lines, and, swapping the parts around, work on them. It will be much more effective if you can learn, rather than read, the lines.

Characters

We learn about the characters in *The Tempest* in a number of ways:

- we observe them in action in situations of calm, of fear, of grief, of intrigue, of mastery, of slavery, of romance
- we have other characters' opinions of them both from twelve years in the past and from the present day
- we learn about them from the way they talk to, and about, others
- we can hear their 'asides', spoken only to themselves and us.

These are just some of the sources from which you can begin, as the play goes on, to form a composite picture of the main characters. Some characters may have contradictory aspects, some may develop or change in the course of the play. All the major characters have been introduced by the end of Act 1.

Start to build up these composite portraits, using whatever information you can obtain. Make sure that you are able to use a short quotation to illustrate and prove each point you make.

Themes

Arising from the discussion points are the main themes we can expect to see developed as the play progresses:

A the power that knowledge, particularly secret knowledge, can give
B the choice between revenge and forgiveness
C basic human behaviour, uninhibited and unthinking, versus civilized, moral behaviour
D the effect that the coloniser has over the existing population and culture
E the power of hate
F the nature of obedience.

Add your contributions to this list.

Close study

Key elements

While scene 1 is important to show the extent of Prospero's power and Ariel's talents, it is scene 2 which needs close attention.

In scene 2 you need to be clear about:

- the major characters, and the light thrown on characters not present
- what happened before the play starts
  - in Milan
  - on the island
- what has happened since
- what motives may influence the action to come
- patterns – both of theme and behaviour – being established now which may recur later in the play.

Scene 2 is long. The important exposition takes place in Prospero's story to Miranda, in his reminder to Ariel of his debt of gratitude and in Caliban's impassioned protest to Prospero. The questions that follow will help you focus on these key elements.

Prospero's story

Act 1 scene 2 lines 66–132

- Prospero decides to tell Miranda their story. Why has she not insisted on hearing it before?
- Why does it seem so terrible to Prospero that the usurper was *'my brother and my uncle'*?
- What is the full significance of *'And to my state grew stranger'* (line 76), *'A confidence sans bound'* (line 97) and *'my library was dukedom large enough'* (line 109)?
- What features of language make Prospero's story sound so fluent and so urgent? For example, check these points:
  - How long are the sentences?
  - How often is there a natural stop at the end of a line? How often in the middle?
  - What effect does the crowding of one verb on another have in lines 110–116?
  - Do you have the impression that this story comes rushing out unplanned, or that Prospero has brooded long on how he will eventually tell it?
  - Does he try to justify what happened?
  - What means does Shakespeare use to prevent this story from being one very long speech?

Ariel's story

Act 1 scene 2 lines 257–296

- Can you suggest why Ariel, who is generally far more articulate than Caliban, has his story told by Prospero?
- What was the connection between Prospero's two servants?
- Ariel – a spirit – is made very physical in this narrative. What images does Shakespeare use to achieve this?
- Over the years Ariel has been portrayed at one end of the scale by women, as a fairy or angel in diaphanous costume and wearing wings or, at the other, as a muscular and near-naked young man. Putting aside any productions of *The Tempest* you may have seen, how would you present Ariel on stage, basing your judgement solely on a close scrutiny of the text of Act 1?

Caliban's story

Act 1 scene 2 lines 330–344

- Prospero's narrative stopped at the moment when he and Miranda reached land. Can you think of a reason?
- Prospero threatens Caliban with torments. Caliban's response is *'I must eat my dinner'*. What does this tell us?
- Prospero said of his brother (line 68) *'he whom...Of all the world I loved'*. Caliban says (line 338) *'and then I lov'd thee'*. What is the pattern that emerges here?
- We learn from what he says that Caliban's sense of loss is his constant preoccupation. How do the vocabulary, the rhythm and even the shape of this speech demonstrate this? Look first at these points and then move on to the detail and phrasing Caliban uses to show his anger and his hurt.

The speech moves from the statement *'This island's mine'* through anecdote, to curses.

- What did Prospero and Miranda provide him with which they later took away?
- What did he give them?
- Pick out the half-sentence which seems to express the essence of slavery.
- Try to enumerate all the losses Caliban has suffered.

Writing

1 Group work

A television play of *The Tempest* is being prepared, and since a long piece of narrative is not considered sufficiently dramatic, Prospero's story to Miranda will be shown as flashback episodes.

Divide the story between members of the group, breaking it down into these three sections:

- Prospero's neglect of his duties, leaving the administration to his brother with all its ensuing temptations, and the conspiracy with Alonso.
- The abduction of Prospero and Miranda at dead of night, with Gonzalo leading the group of men, and the Prince and his sleepy and fretful daughter being put on board ship.
- The two being lowered into a leaky boat, with some provisions. They are driven by wind and wave to the island, make landfall and meet Caliban, who helps them.
- Write the scenario for these episodes. This should include:
  - Scene number
  - Title
  - Setting
  - Characters
  - Key actions (numbered 1, 2, 3 etc.)
  - Key speeches from the play
  - Specifications for long, medium or close-up shots.

Where parts of the story overlap treatment by different groups, you will need to decide together on details for the ongoing characters and setting.

2 One of the underlying themes of this play is that of confinement, or containment. Prospero's threats to Ariel speak of an imprisonment which he has already tasted. Caliban complains of being 'styed'. Prospero was free in Milan – or was he?

Write a short paragraph for each of these three characters in which you investigate what constitutes being 'free' for each of them, what they feel they have lost and gained.

3 'Act 1 scene 2 of *The Tempest* is an unusually lengthy exposition. The drama is mostly in our heads, not where it should be, on the stage.' Do you agree or disagree with this statement?

- Look at the different ways in which we are told what we need to know so that the story can progress.
- How does Shakespeare unfold each of the three stories involving Miranda, Ariel and Caliban?

- Is this approach what scene 1 might have led us to expect?
- Is this how you would have planned to get all this information across if you had been the playwright?

4 What do we learn about the relationship between Prospero and Miranda from their first scene together?

In another part of the island Alonso, his son Sebastian,
Antonio, Prospero's brother, and other members of the royal
party are listening to Gonzalo's attempts to cheer Alonso up.
His theme is that they have been fortunate to escape the
wreck. Alonso, mourning the loss of his son will not be
cheered and the others mock Gonzalo in asides.

3   hint of woe: our unhappy circumstances
5   The masters...merchant: the men in command of some
      merchant ship and the merchant himself who owns it
8–9   weigh...comfort: balance our good and bad fortune
10   He: i.e. Alonso
      cold porridge: there is a pun in 'peace' and porridge.
      Pease-porridge was a soup thickened with dried peas or other
      pulses. It would be kept as a base and added to as necessary.
      Hence the nursery rhyme:
          Pease porridge hot, pease porridge cold
          Pease porridge in the pot, nine days old
11   visitor: (here) someone who visits the sick or bereaved in a
      parish
      give him o'er: give him up so easily
13   strike: a striking mechanism for pocket watches was invented
      about a century before this play was written
15   One. Tell: it has struck one; keep count
18   dollar: in Shakespeare's time 'dollar' was the English name for
      both the German thaler, and the Spanish piece of eight – they
      were both silver coins. Here it is used for 'a sum of money',
      payment. Sebastian plays on the idea that someone who
      'entertains' is a 'performer' who is paid
19   Dolour: pain, grief – again a play on words

- *Throughout this Act, look particularly at the varied
  pace of the scenes and parts of scenes, and how this is
  achieved in the writing.*
- *How does our realisation of what Gonzalo is like
  develop during this scene? Do you find yourself more in
  sympathy with him, or his detractors?*

Act two

Scene 1

The island
Enter ALONSO, SEBASTIAN, ANTONIO, GONZALO,
ADRIAN, FRANCISCO, *and others*

GONZALO	Beseech you sir, be merry; you have cause –
	So have we all – of joy; for our escape
	Is much beyond our loss. Our hint of woe
	Is common; every day, some sailor's wife,
	The masters of some merchant, and the
	merchant, 5
	Have just our theme of woe. But for the miracle –
	I mean our preservation – few in millions
	Can speak like us. Then wisely, good sir, weigh
	Our sorrow with our comfort.
ALONSO	Prithee peace.
SEBASTIAN	He receives comfort like cold porridge. 10
ANTONIO	The visitor will not give him o'er so.
SEBASTIAN	Look, he's winding up the watch of his wit; by and by it will strike.
GONZALO	Sir.
SEBASTIAN	One. Tell. 15
GONZALO	When every grief is entertained that's offered, Comes to th' entertainer –
SEBASTIAN	A dollar.
GONZALO	Dolour comes to him indeed, you have spoken truer than you purposed. 20
SEBASTIAN	You have taken it wiselier than I meant you should.
GONZALO	Therefore my lord –

Gonzalo continues to try to improve Alonso's mood. Antonio and Sebastian continue to make fun of his earnest and kindly efforts. At first these may have been true 'asides' but it becomes plain that they can be heard, as they interrupt Gonzalo.

23 **spendthrift**: someone who spends money extravagantly and wastefully. Here applied to words

24 **I prithee, spare**: Alonso, in his gloom, begs Gonzalo to stop

27 **a good wager**: Antonio and Sebastian have a bet on who will speak next

32 **A laughter**: from the proverb 'He laughs that wins'

34 **Though...desert**: It is Adrian who speaks next, so Antonio wins, laughs, and so is 'paid'
desert: uninhabited

40 **miss 't**: avoid it

41–42 **subtle, tender, and delicate temperance**: gentle, mild and softly temperate climate

43 **Temperance**: Antonio acts as though 'Temperance' – a girl's name – is its meaning here, and so 'delicate' changes its meaning to 'fond of pleasure'

44 **subtle**: applied to a person suggests craftiness

51 **lush and lusty**: tender and vigorous

52 **tawny**: orangey-brown

ANTONIO	Fie, what a spendthrift is he of his tongue.
ALONSO	I prithee, spare.
GONZALO	Well, I have done. But yet –
SEBASTIAN	He will be talking.
ANTONIO	Which, of he or Adrian, for a good wager, first begins to crow?
SEBASTIAN	The old cock.
ANTONIO	The cockerel.
SEBASTIAN	Done. The wager?
ANTONIO	A laughter.
SEBASTIAN	A match.
ADRIAN	Though this island seem to be desert –
ANTONIO	Ha, ha, ha!
SEBASTIAN	So, you're paid.
ADRIAN	Uninhabitable and almost inaccessible –
SEBASTIAN	Yet.
ADRIAN	Yet –
ANTONIO	He could not miss 't.
ADRIAN	It must needs be of subtle, tender, and delicate temperance.
ANTONIO	Temperance was a delicate wench.
SEBASTIAN	Ay, and a subtle; as he most learnedly delivered.
ADRIAN	The air breathes upon us here most sweetly.
SEBASTIAN	As if it had lungs, and rotten ones.
ANTONIO	Or as 't were perfumed by a fen.
GONZALO	Here is everything advantageous to life.
ANTONIO	True; save means to live.
SEBASTIAN	Of that there's none, or little.
GONZALO	How lush and lusty the grass looks! How green!
ANTONIO	The ground indeed is tawny.

25

30

35

40

45

50

The banter continues, with everything that Gonzalo says being subjected to mockery. Gonzalo claims, as Ariel already has, that their clothes seem fresh and bright. Mention of the marriage of Alonso's daughter Claribel to the King of Tunis produces references to the history and mythology of the Dido and Aeneas story in Virgil's *Aeneid*.

53 eye: tinge, shade

55 mistake: picks up the word 'misses' from the previous line

58 As many vouched rarities are: as are many occurrences which are claimed to be rare

60 notwithstanding: in spite of

63 but one of his pockets: even the smallest element in his suit of clothes

65 pocket up: hide, suppress. However, Ariel agrees with Gonzalo (Act 1 scene 2 lines 218–219)

67 Afric: Africa

71–72 a paragon to: perfection as

73 widow Dido: all editors are puzzled by this reference. Dido was Queen of Carthage, a city she had founded. Aeneas, a Trojan prince, fleeing from the ruins of Troy, was driven by a storm on to the shores of Carthage. His wife had died, and he lived with the widowed Dido for some time, until forced to leave by the god Mercury. Dido, in her grief, burnt herself to death on a funeral pyre. There are variants of the story in Greek and Roman mythology, and in Virgil's *Aeneid*. Gonzalo is, to some extent, referring to parallels between this story and that of the group shipwrecked on Prospero's island.

Gonzalo has been bullied, and in rounding on his tormentors, he uses irrelevant detail – 'widow' is hardly a happy turn of phrase just after a wedding ceremony of political significance! He tries to extricate himself from his clumsiness but becomes even more entangled

77 how you take it!: how (quickly) you take him up!

78 You make me study of that: that gives me something to think about

80 This Tunis…Carthage: it was not the same city, but when Carthage was destroyed, Tunis, further along the coast assumed its importance

83 the miraculous harp: a reference to the music of Amphion's harp which 'was so melodious that the stones danced into walls and houses of their own accord' forming the walls of Thebes. Gonzalo has managed to create a whole city

SEBASTIAN	With an eye of green in 't.
ANTONIO	He misses not much.
SEBASTIAN	No; he doth but mistake the truth totally. 55
GONZALO	But the rarity of it is, which is indeed almost beyond credit –
SEBASTIAN	As many vouched rarities are.
GONZALO	That our garments being, as they were, drenched in the sea, hold notwithstanding their freshness and 60 glosses, being rather new-dyed than stained with salt water.
ANTONIO	If but one of his pockets could speak, would it not say he lies?
SEBASTIAN	Ay, or very falsely pocket up his report. 65
GONZALO	Methinks our garments are now as fresh as when we put them on first in Afric, at the marriage of the King's fair daughter Claribel to the King of Tunis.
SEBASTIAN	'Twas a sweet marriage, and we prosper well in our return. 70
ADRIAN	Tunis was never graced before with such a paragon to their queen.
GONZALO	Not since widow Dido's time.
ANTONIO	Widow? A pox o' that! How came that widow in? Widow Dido! 75
SEBASTIAN	What if he had said widower Æneas too? Good Lord, how you take it!
ADRIAN	Widow Dido said you? You make me study of that. She was of Carthage, not of Tunis.
GONZALO	This Tunis sir was Carthage. 80
ADRIAN	Carthage?
GONZALO	I assure you Carthage.
ANTONIO	His word is more than the miraculous harp.
SEBASTIAN	He hath raised the wall, and houses too.

Gonzalo now persists in addressing the King directly, repeating the comment about the freshness of their clothes and recalling that they were first worn at Claribel's wedding. Alonso lashes out, verbally, in his grief at losing his son and having his daughter now so far away. Francisco asserts that Ferdinand may still be alive.

88 kernels: (here) pips, seeds

90 I: some editions have 'Ay' – that is: Gonzalo agreeing with the foregoing conversation. 'I' suggests that Gonzalo is about to start again

91 Why in good time: about time, too!

95 rarest: most excellent

96 Bate...Dido: please leave widow Dido out of it

99 in a sort: to some extent

100 That sort...for: Antonio picks up the word 'sort' as meaning 'lot' (like the modern French 'sort') and suggests that by fishing around among the lots available he got the one he wanted

102–103 You cram...sense: the idea is that Gonzalo is force-feeding Alonso with words he does not want to hear

105 in my rate: as far as I'm concerned, in my opinion

110 beat the surges under him: beat down the waves

112–113 breasted...him: and swam in even the largest waves that rolled in

114 contentious waves: the waves which fought him

114–116 oared...shore: and using his powerful arms like oars, drove himself strongly on to the shore

116 his: i.e. the shore's

wave-worn basis...relieve him: the foot of the cliffs has been eaten away by the waves pounding against it and now appears to bend over the swimmer offering sympathy and help

ANTONIO	What impossible matter will he make easy next? 85
SEBASTIAN	I think he will carry this island home in his pocket, and give it his son for an apple.
ANTONIO	And sowing the kernels of it in the sea, bring forth more islands.
GONZALO	I. 90
ANTONIO	Why in good time.
GONZALO	Sir, we were talking that our garments seem now as fresh as when we were at Tunis at the marriage of your daughter, who is now queen.
ANTONIO	And the rarest that e'er came there. 95
SEBASTIAN	Bate, I beseech you, widow Dido.
ANTONIO	O, widow Dido? Ay, widow Dido.
GONZALO	Is not sir my doublet as fresh as the first day I wore it? I mean, in a sort.
ANTONIO	That sort was well fished for. 100
GONZALO	When I wore it at your daughter's marriage?
ALONSO	You cram these words into mine ears against The stomach of my sense. Would I had never Married my daughter there. For coming thence My son is lost, and, in my rate, she too, 105 Who is so far from Italy removed, I ne'er again shall see her. O thou mine heir Of Naples and of Milan, what strange fish Hath made his meal on thee?
FRANCISCO	Sir he may live. I saw him beat the surges under him, 110 And ride upon their backs. He trod the water, Whose enmity he flung aside, and breasted The surge most swollen that met him. His bold head 'Bove the contentious waves he kept, and oared Himself with his good arms in lusty stroke 115 To the shore, that o'er his wave-worn basis

Sebastian tells Alonso that losing Claribel is his own fault –
his courtiers had begged him not to marry her off to an
African king and she herself only agreed out of duty. Now
his son is lost and there are widows in Milan and Naples
because of the ships he believes are sunk. Gonzalo rebukes
Sebastian for his straight talking.

121 lose: usually spelt 'loose' – the word has overtones of
setting animals to mate. (see *Hamlet* Act 2 scene 2 'I'll
loose my daughter to him')

122 at least: at the very least

123 Who...grief on 't: you who have every reason to weep with
grief about it all
Prithee: I pray thee, please

124–125 importuned otherwise...all of us: and we all begged
you to act differently

126–127 Weighed between...bow: tried to choose between
her unwillingness and obedience, deciding which side of
these scales should go down

128–130 Milan and Naples...comfort them: Milan and Naples
have more widows in them, created by this adventure, than
we can hope to comfort with the few men who return. He
is assuming that they will return and that the rest of the
fleet is lost

131 dear'st: the most precious to Alonso and also the heaviest
loss

134 time: a suitable time
rub the sore: put pressure on the sore

135 the plaster: something to soothe it with
Very well: well said

136 most chirurgeonly: just as a surgeon might (like the
modern French 'chirurgien' – surgeon)

137 foul weather: the different spellings ('fowl' line 138)
suggest a pun but the intention is not clear. It may be that
Sebastian and Antonio are harking back to Gonzalo and
Adrian as cock and cockerel (lines 27–30)

139 Had I plantation: if I had the responsibility for colonising

> • *What light do Sebastian's remarks to Alonso shed on
> father/daughter relationships? How good is the
> relationship between the brothers?*

bowed,
As stooping to relieve him. I not doubt
He came alive to land.

ALONSO   No, no, he's gone.

SEBASTIAN   Sir you may thank yourself for this great loss,
That would not bless our Europe with your
                daughter,   120
But rather lose her to an African;
Where she at least is banished from your eye,
Who hath cause to wet the grief on 't.

ALONSO   Prithee
                peace.

SEBASTIAN   You were kneeled to, and importuned otherwise
By all of us. And the fair soul herself   125
Weighed between loathness and obedience, at
Which end o' the beam should bow. We have lost
                your son,
I fear for ever. Milan and Naples have
Moe widows in them of this business' making
Than we bring men to comfort them.   130
The fault's your own.

ALONSO   So is the dear'st o' th'
                loss.

GONZALO   My lord Sebastian,
The truth you speak doth lack some gentleness,
And time to speak it in. You rub the sore,
When you should bring the plaster.

SEBASTIAN   Very well.   135

ANTONIO   And most chirurgeonly.

GONZALO   It is foul weather in us all, good sir,
When you are cloudy.

SEBASTIAN   Fowl weather?

ANTONIO   Very foul.

GONZALO   Had I plantation of this isle my lord –

Gonzalo suddenly latches on to the notion of being able to organise an ideal colony and develops his ideas to Alonso and the others.

140 **He'd sow 't**: Antonio and Sebastian take the word 'plantation' in the narrower sense of 'planting'
docks, or mallows: docks are broad-leaved weeds usually growing in poor soil in fields or along the roadside. Their leaves cool and soothe nettle stings when laid on them, as do the leaves of the mallow, a tall, flowering plant related to the hollyhock

142 **'Scape**: escape, avoid
want: lack

143 **commonwealth**: state where all the people have a voice and an interest in its organisation

143–144 **by contraries Execute**: carry out everything in the opposite way to that in which it is usually done

144 **traffic**: trade, commerce

145 **admit**: allow
name: (here) office

146 **Letters**: literature, learning

147 **use of service, none**: no one should serve anyone else

148 **Bourn, bound of land**: boundaries. The second phrase serves merely to reinforce the idea
tilth: preparing the soil in order to grow crops, agriculture

152 **king on 't**: king of it. Sebastian comments on Gonzalo's denial of sovereignty because in line 141 he has talked about being king. In the following line Antonio reinforces Sebastian's point

155–156 **All things...endeavour**: nature should be left to produce everything to be shared, without people's work or effort

156 **felony**: crime

157 **pike**: a weapon consisting of a long wooden shaft with an iron (later steel) spike on the end

159 **foison**: abundance – as the next phrase confirms

164 **the golden age**: the first and best age of the world, in which mankind lived in an ideal state of prosperity and happiness. Gonzalo's ideas for the island are taken from Montaigne's essay *De Cannibales* (see page 212)
Save his majesty: (God) the 1690 statute prohibiting swearing on stage may account for the omission of 'God'

> • *Has Gonzalo previously thought these plans through, or are they a sudden inspiration to try to lighten Alonso's gloomy mood?*

ANTONIO	He'd sow 't with nettle-seed.
SEBASTIAN	Or docks, or mallows. 140
GONZALO	And were the king on 't, what would I do?
SEBASTIAN	'Scape being drunk for want of wine.
GONZALO	I' th' commonwealth I would by contraries Execute all things; for no kind of traffic Would I admit; no name of magistrate: 145 Letters should not be known; riches, poverty, And use of service, none: contract, succession, Bourn, bound of land, tilth, vineyard, none; No use of metal, corn, or wine, or oil; No occupation, all men idle, all; 150 And women too, but innocent and pure. No sovereignty.
SEBASTIAN	Yet he would be king on 't.
ANTONIO	The latter end of his commonwealth forgets the beginning.
GONZALO	All things in common nature should produce 155 Without sweat or endeavour. Treason, felony, Sword, pike, knife, gun, or need of any engine, Would I not have. But nature should bring forth Of its own kind, all foison, all abundance, To feed my innocent people. 160
SEBASTIAN	No marrying 'mong his subjects?
ANTONIO	None, man; all idle. Whores and knaves.
GONZALO	I would with such perfection govern sir, T' excel the golden age.
SEBASTIAN	'Save his majesty!
ANTONIO	Long live Gonzalo!
GONZALO	And – do you mark me, sir? 165
ALONSO	Prithee no more. Thou dost talk nothing to me.
GONZALO	I do well believe your Highness, and did it to

As Sebastian and Antonio continue to needle Gonzalo after
he has sketched out his ideal state, Ariel arrives, invisible to
them. Almost immediately Gonzalo, and shortly afterwards
Alonso feel an irresistible drowsiness and fall asleep. So do all
the others except Sebastian and Antonio who are not sleepy
and have undertaken to guard the king.

168 **minister occasion**: give an opportunity (for laughter)

169 **sensible and nimble**: sensitive and active
  they always use: it is their habit

174 **What...there given**: Antonio comments ironically on
  Gonzalo's attempted put-down

175 **An it...flat-long**: if it had not fallen flat. If a blow is made
  with the flat of the sword it does far less damage than the
  sharp edge would

176 **mettle**: spirit. Gonzalo plays on the 'metal' in the sword

176–178 **you would...without changing**: the exact
  significance is not clear. Gonzalo may be saying that if the
  moon stayed in the same orbit long enough they would try
  to steal it. The full moon is popularly associated with
  madness and a five-week moon would be very full indeed –
  so they might be daft enough to try

177 **sphere**: it was thought that the seven planets revolved in
  concentric orbits around the earth – these formed the
  spheres

179 **bat-fowling**: birds were hunted at night. They would fly
  towards a light and be hit with sticks or bats. Sebastian says
  they could use the moon for their lantern

181–182 **adventure...weakly**: risk my reputation for sound
  judgement on such a feeble subject

185–186 **I wish...thoughts**: Alonso wishes that his eyes would
  shut and so shut up his thoughts in sleep

188 **Do not...of it**: do not ignore the serious offer of sleep this
  drowsiness brings

192 **Wondrous**: strangely

> • *Note Antonio's solemn promise to Alonso, his*
> *former partner in crime.*
> • *What thoughts are troubling Alonso? (line 186)*

	minister occasion to these gentlemen, who are of such sensible and nimble lungs that they always use to laugh at nothing. 170
ANTONIO	'Twas you we laughed at.
GONZALO	Who in this kind of merry fooling am nothing to you. So you may continue and laugh at nothing still.
ANTONIO	What a blow was there given.
SEBASTIAN	An it had not fallen flat-long. 175
GONZALO	You are gentlemen of brave mettle; you would lift the moon out of her sphere, if she would continue in it five weeks without changing.

Enter ARIEL, *invisible, playing solemn music*

SEBASTIAN	We would so, and then go a bat-fowling.
ANTONIO	Nay good my lord, be not angry. 180
GONZALO	No I warrant you, I will not adventure my discretion so weakly. Will you laugh me asleep, for I am very heavy?
ANTONIO	Go sleep, and hear us.
	[*All sleep except* ALONSO, SEBASTIAN, *and* ANTONIO
ALONSO	What, all so soon asleep? I wish mine eyes 185 Would, with themselves, shut up my thoughts. I find They are inclined to do so.
SEBASTIAN	Please you sir, Do not omit the heavy offer of it. It seldom visits sorrow; when it doth, It is a comforter.
ANTONIO	We two, my lord, 190 Will guard your person while you take your rest, And watch your safety.
ALONSO	Thank you. Wondrous heavy. [ALONSO *sleeps. Exit* ARIEL
SEBASTIAN	What a strange drowsiness possesses them.

Once Alonso, Gonzalo and the other courtiers are asleep,
Antonio starts suggesting to Sebastian that he could be king.
At first Sebastian does not understand what Antonio is
implying and thinks he must be in a waking dream.

197 **as by consent**: as though by agreement
201 **The occasion speaks thee**: the opportunity prompts you
203 **waking**: awake
210 **wink'st**: find your eyes falling shut
211 **distinctly**: so that I can make out the sense
214 **heed**: pay attention to
215 **Trebles thee o'er**: makes you three times as important
       standing water: water which neither ebbs nor flows

> • *A murderous ambition is being forged. Follow the
>   steps.*

ANTONIO	It is the quality o' th' climate.
SEBASTIAN	Why
	Doth it not then our eyelids sink? I find not 195
	Myself disposed to sleep.
ANTONIO	Nor I, my spirits are
	nimble.
	They fell together all, as by consent;
	They dropp'd, as by a thunder-stroke. What might,
	Worthy Sebastian? O, what might? No more.
	And yet methinks I see it in thy face, 200
	What thou shouldst be. The occasion speaks thee,
	and
	My strong imagination sees a crown
	Dropping upon thy head.
SEBASTIAN	What, art thou
	waking?
ANTONIO	Do you not hear me speak?
SEBASTIAN	I do, and surely
	It is a sleepy language, and thou speak'st 205
	Out of thy sleep. What is it thou didst say?
	This is a strange repose, to be asleep
	With eyes wide open; standing, speaking, moving,
	And yet so fast asleep.
ANTONIO	Noble Sebastian,
	Thou let'st thy fortune sleep – die, rather; wink'st 210
	Whiles thou art waking.
SEBASTIAN	Thou dost snore
	distinctly,
	There's meaning in thy snores.
ANTONIO	I am more serious than my custom. You
	Must be so too, if heed me; which to do
	Trebles thee o'er.
SEBASTIAN	Well, I am standing water. 215
ANTONIO	I'll teach you how to flow.

Antonio persuades Sebastian to agree that Alonso's son,
Ferdinand, has been drowned. They cannot see how he could
possibly have survived. Antonio then asks who is Alonso's
heir if Ferdinand is dead. The answer is Claribel, queen of
Tunis, but she is a long way away.

216–217 To ebb...instructs me: to step back (from fortune) is
my inclination, from a natural laziness. Heredity has also
made him the younger son, so Alonso became king, not
him

218–220 If you...invest it: if you only knew how desirable the
idea is to you, even while you are laughing it off, how in
stripping it bare you clothe it more richly. 'Stripping' and
'invest' both refer to clothes – 'invest' carries the added
significance of a ceremonial or ritual robing, so that the idea
of kingship is being subtly insinuated rather than baldly
stated, and the pictures in Sebastian's mind do at least some
of Antonio's work

220–222 Ebbing men...sloth: men who return to sea with the
current are most often found at the bottom of the flow
because of their cautious fear or their laziness

223–225 The setting...to yield: the expression in your eyes and
the set of your jaw suggest you have something important
to say – something which costs you a lot of effort

226–232 Although...here swims: although this lord of feeble
memory – who will hardly be remembered himself when
he's in his grave – has almost persuaded the King his son is
still alive (he is, after all, a persuader born and bred), this is
as impossible as to suggest that the man sleeping here is
swimming

234–237 No hope...discovery there: no hope in that direction,
looked at another way, is a hope so high that ambition
cannot see beyond it, without being afraid to be found
there. Antonio is persuading Sebastian to have enough
ambition to seize the crown of Naples

241 Ten leagues beyond man's life: so far away as to be
completely out of reach. It can be compared with a phrase
such as 'Dropped off the edge of the world'

SEBASTIAN	Do so. To ebb
	Hereditary sloth instructs me.
ANTONIO	O,
	If you but knew how you the purpose cherish
	Whiles thus you mock it; how in stripping it,
	You more invest it. Ebbing men indeed 220
	Most often do so near the bottom run
	By their own fear or sloth.
SEBASTIAN	Prithee say on.
	The setting of thine eye and cheek proclaim
	A matter from thee, and a birth, indeed,
	Which throes thee much to yield.
ANTONIO	Thus sir. 225
	Although this lord of weak remembrance, this,
	Who shall be of as little memory
	When he is earthed, hath here almost persuaded –
	For he's a spirit of persuasion, only
	Professes to persuade – the King his son's alive, 230
	'Tis as impossible that he's undrowned,
	As he that sleeps here swims.
SEBASTIAN	I have no hope
	That he's undrowned.
ANTONIO	O, out of that no hope
	What great hope have you? No hope that way is
	Another way so high a hope that even 235
	Ambition cannot pierce a wink beyond,
	But doubt discovery there. Will you grant with me
	That Ferdinand is drowned?
SEBASTIAN	He's gone.
ANTONIO	Then
	tell me,
	Who's the next heir of Naples?
SEBASTIAN	Claribel.
ANTONIO	She that is queen of Tunis; she that dwells 240
	Ten leagues beyond man's life; she that from

Antonio points out forcefully that Claribel, the heir of
Naples, if anything should happen to her father, is too far
away for such news to reach her. He asks Sebastian to
imagine his brother were dead, instead of asleep – Gonzalo
too. Sebastian replies cautiously that Antonio supplanted his
brother, Prospero.

242 **no note**: no message
post: the messenger
244 **she that from whom**: Claribel – returning from whose
wedding
245 **some cast again**: some were cast up on shore
246 **destiny**: fate not only saved their lives, but saved them to
carry out the murderous plot he is suggesting
246–248 **to perform...my discharge**: the words 'cast', 'act',
'prologue', 'discharge' are all a play on words used in the
theatre. 'Prologue' is a piece, often in verse, used to
introduce a play; 'discharge' is the performance on stage of
a role. This is a lengthy metaphor
248 **What stuff...say you?**: what are we discussing here? What
are you actually saying?
250–251 **'twixt...some space**: there is a considerable distance
between these cities
251 **cubit**: used here as a vague measure of distance, taken to be
45–55 cm
253 **Measure us**: travel our distance (i.e. the cubits')
Keep: stay
255 **they were**: they would be (if they were dead)
257 **prate**: chatter on aimlessly
259–260 **I myself...deep chat**: I could teach a jackdaw to
chatter at that level
260–262 **O, that you...advancement**: oh, if only you had a
mind like mine, what a sleep this would be to further your
fortunes
263–264 **And how...good fortune?**: how do you rate these
prospects for your own good fortune?
266 **And look...sit upon me**: look how well the clothes of my
station in life suit me

Naples
Can have no note, unless the sun were post –
The man i' th' moon's too slow – till new-born
   chins
Be rough and razorable; she that from whom
We all were sea-swallow'd, though some cast again, 245
And by that destiny to perform an act
Whereof what's past is prologue, what to come
In yours and my discharge.

SEBASTIAN   What stuff is this?
How say you?
'Tis true, my brother's daughter's queen of Tunis;
So is she heir of Naples; 'twixt which regions   250
There is some space.

ANTONIO   A space whose every
   cubit
Seems to cry out, 'How shall that Claribel
Measure us back to Naples? Keep in Tunis,
And let Sebastian wake.' Say, this were death
That now hath seized them; why they were no
   worse   255
Than now they are. There be that can rule
   Naples
As well as he that sleeps; lords that can prate
As amply and unnecessarily
As this Gonzalo. I myself could make
A chough of as deep chat. O, that you bore   260
The mind that I do, what a sleep were this
For your advancement. Do you understand me?

SEBASTIAN   Methinks I do.

ANTONIO   And how does your content
Tender your own good fortune?

SEBASTIAN   I remember
You did supplant your brother Prospero.

ANTONIO   True: 265
And look how well my garments sit upon me,

Antonio's persuasive words gradually work on Sebastian until he agrees. Antonio will kill Alonso and Sebastian will murder Gonzalo. Antonio is sure that the others will not make difficulties. As they are about to draw their swords, Ariel intervenes.

267 **feater**: more neatly

268 **my fellows**: my equals

269 **But for**: what about

270 **kibe**: sore, chilblain on the heel

271 **'Twould...slipper**: I'd have to wear slippers

271–272 **But I feel not...bosom**: this 'god' conscience doesn't bother me at all

273–274 **candied be they...molest**: may they be like sweets and turn sticky and shapeless before they interfere with me

276 **If he were...like**: i.e. if he were dead and turned to earth

279–280 **To the perpetual...ancient morsel**: might put this aged piece of flesh to everlasting sleep

281 **upbraid our course**: rebuke us for what we do

282 **take suggestion**: listen to any evil temptation

283–284 **They'll tell...the hour**: they'll chime with any business we say is best for that moment

287 **the tribute**: Sebastian expresses the practical motive Antonio has for this business, apart from his natural bent for plots and conspiracy

290 **O...word**: just one more thing

291–293 **My master...living**: Ariel's words are addressed to the audience since he would hardly reveal any of Prospero's plans to the enemy. Gonzalo only hears a humming sound

> • *What is the full debt of gratitude that Prospero owes to Gonzalo?*

Much feater than before. My brother's servants
Were then my fellows, now they are my men.

SEBASTIAN   But for your conscience?

ANTONIO   Ay sir, where lies that? If 'twere a kibe,   270
'Twould put me to my slipper. But I feel not
This deity in my bosom. Twenty consciences
That stand 'twixt me and Milan, candied be they,
And melt ere they molest. Here lies your brother,
No better than the earth he lies upon,   275
If he were that which now he's like – that's
     dead –
Whom I with this obedient steel, three inches of it,
Can lay to bed for ever; whiles you doing thus,
To the perpetual wink for aye might put
This ancient morsel, this Sir Prudence, who   280
Should not upbraid our course. For all the rest,
They'll take suggestion as a cat laps milk;
They'll tell the clock to any business that
We say befits the hour.

SEBASTIAN   Thy case, dear friend,
Shall be my precedent. As thou got'st Milan,   285
I'll come by Naples. Draw thy sword; one
     stroke
Shall free thee from the tribute which thou pay'st,
And I the king shall love thee.

ANTONIO   Draw together,
And when I rear my hand, do you the like
To fall it on Gonzalo.

SEBASTIAN   O, but one word.   290
                                          [*They talk apart*

Enter ARIEL, *invisible, with music and song*

ARIEL   My master through his art foresees the danger
That you, his friend, are in; and sends me forth –
For else his project dies – to keep them living.
                                          [*Sings in* GONZALO'S *ear*

Ariel's song wakes up Gonzalo and although he obviously has not heard the words, he is aware of danger. Alonso wakes at the noise and sees the two men with drawn swords. They explain they had heard a roaring as of bulls or lions and had drawn their swords to protect the king. Alonso checks this with Gonzalo who had heard a humming noise. Alonso decides they will go and look for Ferdinand.

295–296 Open-eyed...take: conspiracy, wide awake, seizes the moment
300 good angels: not an order, but a wish 'may good angels...'
302 how now?: what is going on?
303 ghastly: pale and fearful
304 securing your repose: guarding your rest
305 a hollow burst of bellowing: desert islands were recognised to be full of frightening noises – but so is today's countryside to a city dweller; (Caliban in Act 3 scene 2 line 136 says 'The isle is full of noises')

> • *Notice the quick thinking and ensemble playing of Antonio and Sebastian. Gonzalo is still persuading Alonso that his son is on the island. The royal party leaves and Ariel goes to report to Prospero.*

While you here do snoring lie,
Open-eyed conspiracy   295
   His time doth take.
If of life you keep a care,
Shake off slumber, and beware.
   Awake, awake!

ANTONIO   Then let us both be sudden.

GONZALO   [*Wakes*]   Now, good angels 300
Preserve the King.

                                    [*They wake*

ALONSO   Why, how now? Ho, awake! Why are you drawn?
Wherefore this ghastly looking?

GONZALO   What's the
         matter?

SEBASTIAN   Whiles we stood here securing your repose,
Even now, we heard a hollow burst of bellowing   305
Like bulls, or rather lions. Did 't not wake you?
It struck mine ear most terribly.

ALONSO   I heard nothing.

ANTONIO   O, 'twas a din to fright a monster's ear,
To make an earthquake; sure it was the roar
Of a whole herd of lions.

ALONSO   Heard you this,
         Gonzalo?   310

GONZALO   Upon mine honour, sir, I heard a humming,
And that a strange one too, which did awake me.
I shaked you sir, and cried. As mine eyes opened,
I saw their weapons drawn. There was a noise,
That's verily. 'Tis best we stand upon our guard,   315
Or that we quit this place. Let's draw our
         weapons.

ALONSO   Lead off this ground, and let's make further search
For my poor son.

GONZALO   Heavens keep him from these
         beasts.

Elsewhere on the island, to the sound of an approaching storm, Caliban is fetching wood. To himself he mutters curses on Prospero and lists some of the torments he himself is subjected to. Seeing Trinculo, a jester, he assumes that he is one of Prospero's spirits and lies flat on the ground, hoping he will not be noticed. Trinculo is looking for shelter.

 2 **flats**: swamps. It was a popular idea that the sun drew up various types of water vapour and let them fall again. Some country people, when shafts of sunlight slant down through stormclouds, still tell children 'the sun is drawing up water'
 3 **By inch-meal**: inch by inch
 5 **urchin-shows**: goblins appearing like hedgehogs
   pitch me i' th' mire: throw me in the mud
 6 **firebrand**: presumably a will-o'-the-wisp
 8 **every trifle**: the least offence
 9 **mow**: make faces
13 **wound**: entwined
   cloven: forked
17 **mind**: notice
18 **bear off**: keep off

> • *Look closely at the life Caliban is forced to lead. It appears not only in what he says but in the way he acts.*

For he is sure i' th' island.

ALONSO   Lead away.

ARIEL: Prospero my lord shall know what I have done.   320
And yet So, King, go safely on to seek thy son.

[*Exeunt*

Scene 2

The island

Enter CALIBAN *with a burden of wood. A noise of
thunder heard*

CALIBAN   All the infections that the sun sucks up
From bogs, fens, flats, on Prosper fall, and make
    him
By inch-meal a disease. His spirits hear me,
And yet I needs must curse. But they'll nor pinch,
Fright me with urchin-shows, pitch me i' th'
    mire,   5
Nor lead me, like a firebrand, in the dark
Out of my way, unless he bid 'em; but
For every trifle are they set upon me;
Sometime like apes, that mow and chatter at me,
And after bite me, then like hedgehogs, which   10
Lie tumbling in my barefoot way, and mount
Their pricks at my footfall. Sometime am I
All wound with adders, who with cloven tongues
Do hiss me into madness.

Enter TRINCULO

                            Lo, now lo,
Here comes a spirit of his, and to torment me   15
For bringing wood in slowly. I'll fall flat,
Perchance he will not mind me.

TRINCULO   Here's neither bush nor shrub to bear off any
weather at all, and another storm brewing; I hear it

Trinculo realises that a storm is imminent and is looking for shelter. At first he thinks Caliban must be a kind of fish, partly because of the smell. He then realises he is a man and decides there is nothing for it but to creep under Caliban's coat. When he is hidden, the drunken Stephano, a butler, appears, singing.

21 bombard: the earliest kind of cannon and then a leather jug for holding liquor. It was coated with tar and was also called a 'black-jack'

27 Poor-John: salted and dried hake

28–30 Were I...piece of silver: if he'd had a signboard painted to suggest what people might see, he could have exhibited Caliban in a tent for the holiday crowds to pay to gawp at. People with some extraordinary feature, either real or contrived, were shown at fairs in this way, until the middle of the twentieth century

30–31 There would...a man: both be seen as a man, but a strange one and make the exhibitor a fortune

32 doit: a small coin of very low value

34 a dead Indian: indigenous people of the newly 'discovered' New World countries were brought back by leaders of these expeditions in the sixteenth century. They were exhibited to the paying public alive or dead. They tended not to live long in the conditions under which they were kept

34–35 Legged...arms: Trinculo continues his investigation of Caliban

37 lately suffered by a thunderbolt: recently killed when lightning struck him. It was believed that something like an arrow striking the victim was the cause of death on these occasions

39 gaberdine: a loose coat or cloak

41 shroud: take shelter

42 dregs: a reference to the last remnants of the wine being poured from the bombard

45 This is a very scurvy tune: this is a pretty rotten song

47 swabber: a sailor who cleans (swabs) the decks

51 a tongue with a tang: a sharp tongue

> • *Caliban is exploited in his native land and would possibly be treated worse abroad. What future is there for him? This question will be worth considering again at the end of Act 5.*

sing i' th' wind. Yond same black cloud, yond   20
huge one, looks like a foul bombard that would
shed his liquor. If it should thunder as it did before,
I know not where to hide my head. Yond same
cloud cannot choose but fall by pailfuls. What have
we here? A man or a fish? Dead or alive? A fish: 25
he smells like a fish. A very ancient and fish-like
smell. A kind of, not of the newest Poor-John. A
strange fish. Were I in England now, as once I was,
and had but this fish painted, not a holiday fool
there but would give a piece of silver. There   30
would this monster make a man. Any strange beast
there makes a man. When they will not give a doit
to relieve a lame beggar, they will lay out ten to see
a dead Indian. Legged like a man. And his fins like
arms. Warm, o' my troth. I do now let loose my   35
opinion, hold it no longer, this is no fish, but an
islander, that hath lately suffered by a thunderbolt.
[*Thunder*] Alas, the storm is come again. My best
way is to creep under his gaberdine; there is no
other shelter hereabout. Misery acquaints a man   40
with strange bed-fellows. I will here shroud till the
dregs of the storm be past.

Enter STEPHANO, *singing: a bottle in his hand*

STEPHANO   I shall no more to sea, to sea,
                          Here shall I die ashore –
                  This is a very scurvy tune to sing at a man's   45
                  funeral. Well, here's my comfort.   [*Drinks*
                  [*Sings*]
                      The master, the swabber, the boatswain, and I,
                          The gunner, and his mate
                      Loved Mall, Meg, and Marian, and Margery,
                          But none of us cared for Kate.   50
                          For she had a tongue with a tang,
                          Would cry to a sailor, Go hang!
                      She loved not the savour of tar nor of pitch,

Stephano, drinking wine and singing hears Caliban who, thinking he is one of Prospero's spirits, begs him not to torment him. Stephano sees four legs, two are Trinculo's, and, assuming Caliban is a monster, plans to take him back to Naples after curing his 'fit' with drink.

54 scratch her...itch: satisfy her urge for sex

59 put tricks upon 's: play tricks with us
men of Ind: American Indians

61–62 as proper...four legs: Stephano has adapted the 'two legs' of the proverb to 'four' to fit the situation

64 at': at the

67 ague: in fevers where the patient alternates between cold and hot, the cold shaking fit is the ague

69 recover him: make him well

72 neat's leather: cowhide, the skin of calves or cows, tanned to make leather

75–76 after the wisest: in the most sensible way

77 go near to: go a long way to

78–80 I will not...that soundly: the suggestion is that he will not put too high a price on him – but the highest offer will win him

81 anon: soon

82 thy trembling: Trinculo is trembling with fear. To Caliban, Prospero may seem the same when he is angry or conjuring spirits

85 cat: from the proverb which says liquor will make a cat speak

	Yet a tailor might scratch her where'er she did itch.
	Then to sea, boys, and let her go hang 55
	This is a scurvy tune too; but here's my comfort.
	[Drinks

CALIBAN   Do not torment me, O!

STEPHANO   What's the matter? Have we devils here? Do you put tricks upon 's with savages, and men of Ind, ha? I have not 'scaped drowning to be afeard now of 60 your four legs. For it hath been said, as proper a man as ever went on four legs cannot make him give ground. And it shall be said so again while Stephano breathes at' nostrils.

CALIBAN   The spirit torments me. Oh!   65

STEPHANO   This is some monster of the isle with four legs, who hath got, as I take it, an ague. Where the devil should he learn our language? I will give him some relief, if it be but for that. If I can recover him, and keep him tame, and get to Naples with him, 70 he's a present for any emperor that ever trod on neat's leather.

CALIBAN   Do not torment me prithee. I'll bring my wood home faster.

STEPHANO   He's in his fit now, and does not talk after the 75 wisest. He shall taste of my bottle. If he have never drunk wine afore, it will go near to remove his fit. If I can recover him, and keep him tame, I will not take too much for him; he shall pay for him that hath him, and that soundly.   80

CALIBAN   Thou dost me yet but little hurt; thou wilt anon, I know it by thy trembling. Now Prosper works upon thee.

STEPHANO   Come on your ways. Open your mouth. Here is that which will give language to you, cat. Open 85 your mouth; this will shake your shaking, I can tell

Stephano pours wine into Caliban's mouth. Trinculo thinks
he recognises Stephano's voice but is scared because he is
sure Stephano must be dead. Stephano, hearing a voice from
the other end of the monster tries to give it drink as well.
Trinculo and Stephano recognise each other. Caliban thinks
Stephano, the provider of such drink, is a god.

88 **chaps**: chops, jaws
91 **a most delicate monster**: a very special monster, I must say
94 **detract**: disparage, speak ill of (his friend)
95 **Amen**: (here) that's enough
100 **no long spoon**: from the proverbial idea that 'he who sups
with the devil needs a long spoon'
101 **beest**: present subjunctive of 'to be'. The modern usage is
'if you are'
107 **siege**: (here) excrement (more usually 'seat' or 'stool')
moon-calf: 'an inanimate shapeless mass – an abortion,
supposed to be produced by the influence of the moon'.
Also 'a born fool'
108 **vent**: defecate
116 **constant**: steady
117 **an if they be not sprites**: as long as they are not spirits.
Spirits to Caliban are creatures at Prospero's command
which torment him

you, and that soundly. You cannot tell who's your
friend. Open your chaps again.

TRINCULO   I should know that voice. It should be – but he is
drowned; and these are devils. O defend me!   90

STEPHANO   Four legs and two voices – a most delicate monster.
His forward voice now is to speak well of his friend;
his backward voice is to utter foul speeches, and to
detract. If all the wine in my bottle will recover
him, I will help his ague. Come. Amen, I will   95
pour some in thy other mouth.

TRINCULO   Stephano.

STEPHANO   Doth thy other mouth call me? Mercy, mercy! This
is a devil, and no monster: I will leave him, I have
no long spoon.   100

TRINCULO   Stephano. If thou beest Stephano, touch me, and
speak to me; for I am Trinculo – be not afeard – thy
good friend Trinculo.

STEPHANO   If thou beest Trinculo, come forth. I'll pull thee by
the lesser legs. If any be Trinculo's legs, these   105
are they. Thou art very Trinculo indeed. How
camest thou to be the siege of this moon-calf? Can
he vent Trinculos?

TRINCULO   I took him to be killed with a thunder-stroke. But
art thou not drowned Stephano? I hope now   110
thou art not drowned. Is the storm overblown? I
hid me under the dead moon-calf's gaberdine for
fear of the storm. And art thou living Stephano? O
Stephano, two Neapolitans 'scaped!

STEPHANO   Prithee do not turn me about, my stomach is   115
not constant.

CALIBAN   These be fine things, an if they be not sprites.
That 's a brave god, and bears celestial liquor.
I will kneel to him.

STEPHANO   How didst thou 'scape? How camest thou   120
hither? Swear by this bottle how thou camest

Stephano had escaped from the wreck on a barrel of wine. Trinculo tells him that he swam ashore. Caliban is so impressed with the wine that he swears to become Stephano's subject. He thinks Stephano has come from heaven and Stephano plays up to this. Caliban offers to show Stephano some of the secrets of the island and regards him as a god.

122 butt of sack: barrel of wine. 'Sack' usually referred to white wines imported from Spain and the Canaries, and possibly originated in the French word 'sec' – dry

131 kiss the book: a reference to kissing the Bible when swearing an oath and kissing the cup when drinking to someone

138 Out o' th' moon: some colonists played on the superstition of natives by making this claim. Compare this with the claims sometimes made today, by allegedly more sophisticated people, of visitations from outer space

139 when time was: once upon a time

141–142 thee...thy bush: people have always tried to make out shapes on the moon. Either it looks like a whole face, or traditionally a man with a dog and carrying a thornbush. Tradition says it is a man carrying sticks picked up on a Sunday, or Cain, the first murderer, who killed his brother Abel

143–144 I will...new contents: I will refill the bottle from the cask I have hidden

148 Well drawn: a good draught of wine

149–150 I'll show thee...god: Caliban seems to be making again what he has bitterly perceived to be an error of judgement he made with Prospero (Act 1 scene 2 lines 336–339)

hither. I escaped upon a butt of sack, which the
sailors heaved o'erboard, by this bottle which I
made of the bark of a tree with mine own hands,
since I was cast ashore.   125

CALIBAN   I'll swear upon that bottle, to be thy true subject,
for the liquor is not earthly.

STEPHANO   Here. Swear then how thou escapedst.

TRINCULO   Swum ashore, man, like a duck. I can swim like a
duck, I'll be sworn.   130

STEPHANO   Here, kiss the book. Though thou canst swim like
a duck, thou art made like a goose.

TRINCULO   O Stephano, hast any more of this?

STEPHANO   The whole butt, man; my cellar is in a rock by the
sea-side, where my wine is hid. How now   135
moon-calf, how does thine ague?

CALIBAN   Hast thou not dropped from heaven?

STEPHANO   Out o' th' moon, I do assure thee. I was the man i'
th' moon when time was.

CALIBAN   I have seen thee in her, and I do adore thee.   140
My mistress showed me thee, and thy dog, and thy
bush.

STEPHANO   Come, swear to that. Kiss the book. I will furnish it
anon with new contents. Swear.

TRINCULO   By this good light, this is a very shallow   145
monster. I afeard of him? A very weak monster. The
man i' th' moon. A most poor credulous monster.
Well drawn monster, in good sooth.

CALIBAN   I'll show thee every fertile inch o' th' island.
And I will kiss thy foot. I prithee be my god.   150

TRINCULO   By this light, a most perfidious and drunken
monster. When 's god's asleep, he'll rob his bottle.

CALIBAN   I'll kiss thy foot. I'll swear myself thy subject.

STEPHANO   Come on then. Down, and swear.

TRINCULO   I shall laugh myself to death at this puppy-   155

Caliban has seized the chance to escape Prospero's tyranny
by offering what were once his secrets to the newcomer,
Stephano. Stephano, assuming that the King and all the rest
are dead, says that he and Trinculo will inherit the island.

161–162 I'll show thee...wood enough: colonists often
depended on the local population for the means of life until
things changed; either the colonists grew greedy or the
natives became disenchanted with their ways

168 crabs: crab apples, small wild apples or crabs, the
crustaceans

169 pig-nuts: also called earth-nuts or earth chestnuts – an
edible tuber which grows wild in parts of Britain. According
to an eighteenth century book about herbs they 'provoke
lust exceedingly', which might help to account for Caliban's
attempt on Miranda

171 marmoset: a small monkey, apparently good to eat

172 filberts: hazel nuts

173 young scamels: no one is sure what a scamel is. Since its
habitat is rocks, it is either bird, fish or shellfish. Perhaps the
clue lies in the adjective 'young' which is most likely to
apply to a young and therefore tender bird. Fish and
shellfish are usually more prized for their large size.
'Sea-mel' or sea-mew – a type of gull would fit this theory

177 fill him: either fill the bottle, or fill Caliban

182 firing: kindling or wood for the fire

184 trenchering: a trencher was originally a flat piece of wood
used as a plate. The addition of '-ing' turns it into a
collective noun

185 'Ban, 'Ban, Cacaliban: 'Ban' a shortening of Caliban and
'Cacaliban' a lengthening of it, possibly with a drunken
hiccup

186 Get a new man: presumably addressed to Prospero.
Caliban meets another man with designs on the island.
What mistake is he about to repeat?

187 high-day: a day of celebration, a holiday

	headed monster. A most scurvy monster. I could find in my heart to beat him –	
STEPHANO	Come, kiss.	
TRINCULO	But that the poor monster's in drink. An abominable monster.	160
CALIBAN	I'll show thee the best springs. I'll pluck thee berries. I'll fish for thee, and get thee wood enough. A plague upon the tyrant that I serve; I'll bear him no more sticks, but follow thee, Thou wondrous man.	165
TRINCULO	A most ridiculous monster, to make a wonder of a poor drunkard.	
CALIBAN	I prithee let me bring thee where crabs grow; And I with my long nails will dig thee pig-nuts; Show thee a jay's nest, and instruct thee how To snare the nimble marmoset. I'll bring thee To clustering filberts, and sometimes I'll get thee Young scamels from the rock. Wilt thou go with me?	170
STEPHANO	I prithee now lead the way without any more talking. Trinculo, the King and all our company else being drowned, we will inherit here. Here, bear my bottle. Fellow Trinculo, we'll fill him by and by again.	175
CALIBAN	[*Sings drunkenly*] Farewell master; farewell, farewell.	
TRINCULO	A howling monster; a drunken monster.	180
CALIBAN	No more dams I'll make for fish, Nor fetch in firing At requiring; Nor scrape trenchering, nor wash dish. 'Ban, 'Ban, Cacaliban Has a new master. Get a new man. Freedom, high-day, high-day, freedom, freedom, high-day, freedom!	185
STEPHANO	O brave monster. Lead the way. [*Exeunt*	

Keeping track

Scene 1

1 What reasoning does Gonzalo use to put a brave face on their situation?
2 How does Alonso respond to Gonzalo's attempts to cheer him up?
3 How do Antonio and Sebastian react to Gonzalo's efforts?
4 What has Gonzalo noticed about their clothes?
5 What are the two main reasons for Alonso's grief?
6 Is there any evidence to show Alonso and Sebastian that Ferdinand may have survived the wreck?
7 What is Sebastian's attitude to Alonso's 'loss' of his daughter Claribel?
8 Why does Ariel, on Prospero's orders, allow only Antonio and Sebastian to stay awake?
9 What are Antonio's motives – obvious and perhaps less obvious – for suggesting murder to Sebastian? How willing is Sebastian to agree?
10 How do they explain their drawn swords to Alonso and Gonzalo when Ariel wakes them up?

Scene 2

1 Why does Caliban hide when he thinks Trinculo is one of Prospero's spirits?
2 How does it happen that Stephano finds a four-legged monster with two voices?
3 What would Stephano and Trinculo do with Caliban, given the opportunity?
4 How did Stephano escape the wreck? What about Trinculo?
5 How does Stephano justify his 'right' to the island?
6 What effect does the wine have on Caliban?
7 What does Caliban offer Stephano and Trinculo, and what does he expect in exchange?

Discussion

Prospero and Miranda have come to terms with the island over the years. The royal party has just arrived after surviving a violent shipwreck. They have been greatly removed from their normal circumstances.

A *Scene 1*

1 What do you think the standard of living would have been at the court of Naples?
2 What behaviour would you expect at court between the King, the brother to the King, the councillor to the King, the Duke of Milan and the courtiers in the presence of the King? In what ways do they seem to behave out of role now? How do you account for the quite cruel treatment of the 'honest old councillor' Gonzalo?
3 If you had been shipwrecked with others in a completely alien environment what do you think your first reactions would be? What would you do if you had lost a much-loved member of your family, or a friend, in the wreck? Does anything seem strange about their concerns?
4 We know from Ariel (Act 1 scene 2 lines 217–219) that *'Not a hair perished'* and that their clothes were *'fresh'*. How do they treat Gonzalo's remark about their clothes? Why do you think they have not observed for themselves the unlikely state they and their clothes are in?
5 What does Sebastian's outburst (lines 118–130) suggest about the true state of Alonso's popularity and authority at court?
6 Why do you think Gonzalo wants to organise his ideal community *'by contraries'*?
7 What is attractive to Antonio about first suggesting his murderous plot to Sebastian on what appears to him to be a desert island?
8 What is it which finally makes the royal party act together, as a group of human beings at risk?
9 Prospero has flourished on the island, thanks in part at least to an absence of constraint. In your judgement has this same quality had a good or bad effect on the royal party?

Scene 2

1 How do you feel about Caliban after his first speech in this scene?
2 Prospero has made Caliban his slave and Caliban now sees him as a tyrant. What is similar in the initial stages of Prospero's approach to Caliban and that of Stephano and Trinculo? How does the idea of Stephano and Trinculo's superiority over him develop in Caliban's mind?
3 Why do you think Caliban now sees himself as a willing subject? Do you feel that Trinculo and Stephano are likely to be better masters than Prospero?
4 Does Caliban have anything in common with Stephano and Trinculo?

B   In Act 2, two people, Gonzalo and Stephano, fantasise about being in charge of an island. More detailed plans of Stephano's intentions appear in Act 3, but Gonzalo lays out his ideas here.

Gonzalo

1   Parts of the 'New World' (new to the explorers of course, not to the indigenous population) were being colonised at about the time this play was being written (see Possible sources, page 217). Gonzalo is talking about a populated island. He may be thinking that 'this isle' has a native population they are not yet aware of or he may intend to populate it with settlers eager to make a fresh start. What differences will he face in either case, compared with the situation Prospero found and dealt with?

2   Gonzalo has decided to organise things *'by contraries'*. Do you think it will work? What questions would you like to put to him? What is the central confusion in Gonzalo's vision of this ideal commonwealth which Sebastian and Antonio comment on?

Character

Act 2 offers many insights into the characters, and several pointers will have arisen in the course of your discussions. It is worth investigating these:

- We had a first impression of Antonio and Sebastian in the storm. Are our feelings about them confirmed here?
- By the time Ariel enters in scene 1 what have we learnt about Gonzalo's character and attitudes?
- In scene 2 we meet Stephano and Trinculo for the first time and learn a great deal about them. Look carefully at what they say and do when they are alone, together, and with Caliban. Can you differentiate between the two of them?
- In scene 2 we also have a 'window' on Caliban's life as he sees it. Does this alter your earlier impressions of this character?

It will help you if you keep your character notes up to date. Fresh first impressions can be useful and are an important basis on which to build. It is equally useful to have to reassess them in the light of later evidence.

Drama

A   In Scene 1 lines 143–164 we hear Gonzalo's manifesto for a brave new world. In two groups, X and Y, prepare for a press conference.

- Group X consists of Gonzalo and his political colleagues, idealists who believe passionately in this point of view.
- Group Y is made up of sceptical political and other journalists who think the whole idea is deeply flawed.

Both groups should prepare for the press conference by looking for the points which are most susceptible to attack. Some examples of possible questions to consider:

1   If there are no laws, how will any disputes be resolved?
2   If there is no trade, how will fair distribution of food and other essentials be ensured?
3   It is a good idea to avoid a hierarchy based on wealth and poverty, on master and servant. This should lessen any feelings of resentment and so reduce conflict. Are there other kinds of hierarchy which might develop?
4   If there are no positions of prestige to aim for, will ambition die out?
5   Will this society be better or worse for women?
6   Sebastian's remark (Act 2 scene 1 line 141) suggests that Gonzalo is known to disapprove of wine-drinking. Since even quite unsophisticated societies make beer from millet or root vegetables, will it be possible to ban it? Will it even be desirable to do so?

We have seen how easy it is to ridicule Gonzalo's ideas mindlessly. Group X should structure their plans as far as possible and the journalists should make sure they put constructive questions.

B   Comedy … is hard to do! Study the first appearance of Stephano and Trinculo. These clowns are sometimes played on stage by professional comics. It is their mastery of timing, gesture, voice and mime which combine to make us laugh. In Shakespeare's comic scenes it is often difficult to see from the printed page what is likely to be funny. They have to be acted.

In this scene (Act 2 scene 2) there is one sustained visual gag and a lot of drunkenness.

- Work in pairs or threes.
- Choose a short section of no more than about twenty lines, which looks promising to you.
- Try to work it into an amusing sketch.
- Add any gags or props or topical jokes – even changing Shakespeare's words slightly as long as you make it funny.
- Try it on the rest of the group.

Close study

Scene 1

A Gonzalo's first speech is meant to cheer up Alonso, who is mourning the loss of his only son and heir.

1 It does not have the desired effect. Why not?
2 Pick out words and phrases which you would not use in similar circumstances, and explain your reasons.
3 This speech and Alonso's reply immediately lay Gonzalo open to ridicule. What might be behind Sebastian's and Antonio's reactions?

B Look at the various ways in which Antonio and Sebastian comment on and belittle Gonzalo's efforts. Find examples, with line references, of the following methods of theirs:

1 Anticipating what Gonzalo will say or do next
2 Interrupting
3 Taking over the conversation entirely for a while
4 Using a punning reference to distract attention from what is really being said
5 Laying bets on who will speak next
6 Openly contradicting what has been said
7 Ridicule

C It is no good thinking of clever replies five minutes later! Work in threes. Take a short section of this part of the scene where you are happy that you understand the references, and work out:

1 Just how fast these exchanges need to be.
2 How the key words can be pointed up without being heavy-handed.
3 How Antonio and Sebastian work together to make these interventions tell.

Perform your extract for the rest of the group.

D We have learnt from Prospero's story to Miranda that Gonzalo was put in charge of their murderous exile from Milan – a task which appears to be quite against his nature. He may also be the only character in the play with a wife and children whom he loves (Act 1 scene 1 line 59).

1 What reflections of his character and experience can you find in his hopes for an ideal society?

E Once Alonso, Gonzalo and the others are asleep the tone changes. It only takes a glance at the page to see that Antonio has the longest speeches he has had yet; Sebastian has short questions and comments. This is serious persuasion.

This part of the scene can conveniently be looked at in four segments:

1 Lines 196–212

2 Lines 213–225

3 Lines 226–262

4 Lines 263–289

Read each segment carefully, in sequence, and decide what themes are the main characteristic of each of them.

1 • Look for words which can suggest both sleep and death.
   • Look for unfinished suggestions left hanging (lines 198–201).
   • Look for Antonio's 'vision' of what might be.

2 • In line 213 how does Antonio make the break between what has gone before and what is to follow?
   • Why is it appropriate for Antonio to set himself up as a teacher?
   • Sebastian (lines 217–221) appears to treat too lightly what Antonio is trying to propose to him. How does Antonio interpret this attitude?

3 • How does Antonio dispose of the question of succession to the crown?
   • Is Sebastian just slow to see his advantage, or is he more honest than Antonio?
   • Find the line where Sebastian finally realises he is talking to an expert.

4 • Sebastian puts the all-important question about conscience, since Antonio has faced up to this before. What does Antonio's answer tell us about him? How does the imagery he uses emphasise this? You will need to look at this speech again in the last scene of the play.
   • What effect do you think the distancing of Gonzalo in the earlier part of the scene and name-calling like that in line 280 may have had on Sebastian's decision?
   • What is Sebastian now offering Antonio in return for his services?
   • How does the imagery of lines 273–281 echo that at the beginning of the scene? What effect has the repetition of this theme had on Sebastian, and what effect on the audience?

Scene 2

1 For the first time we see Caliban on his own and hear the proof that he has learnt to curse. What experiences are his curses based on?

2 Two observations of his (in lines 4–7) show that he is capable of learning. What has he learnt about Prospero's spirits?

3 In this speech he speaks in lists: of nouns (line 2); of verbs (lines 4–7); of longer phrases describing his torments (lines 9–14). Why does he do this, and what effect does it have on us, the audience?

4 Trinculo is a court jester. What elements in his first speech, as he investigates what is under the coat, suggest his occupation? He is not drunk, but what imagery suggests very early on that drink is not far from his mind?

5 Stephano is drunk. In what ways is this shown? How does Caliban's opening speech, which could have been seen to stand alone, continue to feed through this part of the scene (lines 57–83)?

6 Comedy, and at the same time quite moving comedy, is made by the reunion of Trinculo and Stephano, who had thought each other dead. Think about your own good friendships. How does Shakespeare create this rather jokey and relaxed relationship? You will need to look at the words, the turns of phrase, the exclamations and the actions – those suggested in the text (for example line 104) and those that the situation invites you to add. Make a list of separate points for what you discover.

7 Caliban started this scene and ends it. What is his mood now? Is this just because he is drunk? What qualities in Caliban do the lines 161–165 and 168–173 show? What is remarkable about his possession of these qualities at this stage?

Key scene

Scene 1

The questions and comments in Key scene assume that you have at least worked through the Close study questions relating to that scene. You will find it useful to make notes on your thoughts, ideas and questions, as you study each key scene.

1 The inner circle of the Naples court has been removed to a desert island. What has this meant for:
  • Alonso's position?
  • Gonzalo's position?

- What do we learn about Alonso's, Antonio's and Sebastian's powers of:
  - leadership
  - maturity
  - loyalty
  - civility
  - humanity
  - family feeling?
2 From Prospero's remarks to Miranda in Act 1 we see that he is ready to make some excuses for Antonio's behaviour twelve years previously. What do we know now about Antonio's attitude to:
- weakness
- ambition
- the crown
- money
- social position
- power
- corruption
- murder
- conscience
- remorse?

Writing

1 In old age Sebastian comes to write his memoirs. He still has an almost photographic memory of the moment when Antonio persuaded him to take part in the murder of Alonso and Gonzalo. Look carefully at the scene and review the subtle (and not so subtle) steps in the process. Write this part of Sebastian's memoirs and decide from Sebastian's point of view how the persuasion worked on him.
2 Prospero and Miranda hate and despise Caliban. Stephano and Trinculo find him strange and amusing. Write a balanced character study of him so far, firmly based on the text.
3 Act 2 is remarkable for the variety achieved in the writing. Write three paragraphs in which you comment, using appropriate quotations, on the purposes for which Shakespeare uses:
- short lines and part-lines
- longer speeches
- soliloquies (see GLOSSARY page 226).

Prospero has set Ferdinand the task of carrying logs, which
Caliban usually has to do. Ferdinand is claiming to himself
that even this hard chore is tolerable as long as he can think of
Miranda. She comes to tell him that it is safe to talk as her
father is in his study. Unknown to them, he is actually
observing them.

1–2 **There be...sets off**: some sports and occupations which
 require effort and even pain, reward this with the pleasure they
 provide
 2 **baseness**: menial tasks
 3 **most poor**: the poorest actions
 4 **mean**: inferior, petty
 5 **as odious**: as disagreeable
 6 **which**: whom
 quickens: brings to life
 8 **crabbed**: bad-tempered, churlish
 11 **Upon a sore injunction**: under the threat of severe
 punishment
 12–13 **such baseness...executor**: such hard labour was never
 carried out by someone of my standing
 15 **Most busilest, when I do it**: everything that Ferdinand has
 said so far in this scene has insisted that pleasant thoughts of
 his love, Miranda, make his hard labour easier to bear. This
 means that readings 'lest' and 'least' turn this meaning on its
 head. One suggestion is that the reading 'busilest' means
 'busiest', so that Ferdinand is still claiming that when he is
 hardest at work, his thoughts of Miranda refresh him most
 happily
 19 **'Twill weep**: particularly if the wood is pine (as in 'cloven pine'
 Act 1 scene 2 line 277) then drops of resin will run from it like
 tears as it burns
 21 **He's safe**: he is safely out of our way

• *What is Prospero hoping to learn?*

Act three

Scene

Near PROSPERO'S *cell*

Enter FERDINAND, *bearing a log*

FERDINAND   There be some sports are painful, and their labour
Delight in them sets off. Some kinds of baseness
Are nobly undergone, and most poor matters
Point to rich ends. This my mean task
Would be as heavy to me as odious, but   5
The mistress which I serve quickens what's dead,
And makes my labours pleasures. O she is
Ten times more gentle than her father's crabbed,
And he's composed of harshness. I must remove
Some thousands of these logs, and pile them up, 10
Upon a sore injunction. My sweet mistress
Weeps when she sees me work, and says, such
          baseness
Had never like executor. I forget.
But these sweet thoughts do even refresh my labours
Most busiest, when I do it.

Enter MIRANDA; *and* PROSPERO *at a distance, unseen*

MIRANDA   Alas, now pray you 15
Work not so hard. I would the lightning had
Burnt up those logs that you are enjoined to pile.
Pray, set it down and rest you. When this burns,
'Twill weep for having wearied you. My father
Is hard at study; pray now rest yourself: 20
He's safe for these three hours.

FERDINAND   O most dear
          mistress,

Miranda offers to help Ferdinand and let him rest. He
refuses. Prospero sees that Miranda is infatuated. When
Ferdinand learns her name he tells her she is the most perfect
woman he has met.

22–23 before I shall...to do: before I shall have finished the
task which has been set me

28–29 become me...does you: be as suitable for me as for you

31 worm: (here) an expression of affection or tenderness

32 visitation: (here) visit, with the additional meanings of
'plague', 'infection' and visiting the sick or bereaved. They
are, after all, both 'love-sick'

37 hest: instruction. Prospero had ordered her not to tell
Ferdinand her name

Admired: a play on the name Miranda

39 dearest: most valuable, most precious

41–42 The harmony...too diligent ear: the charming things
they have said have enslaved me for listening to them too
devotedly

45 owed: owned

46 And put it to the foil: and fought with it. (Foils are used in
fencing)

47 peerless: unequalled

	The sun will set before I shall discharge	
	What I must strive to do.	
MIRANDA	If you'll sit down,	
	I'll bear your logs a while. Pray give me that;	
	I'll carry it to the pile.	
FERDINAND	No, precious creature,	25
	I had rather crack my sinews, break my back,	
	Than you should such dishonour undergo,	
	While I sit lazy by.	
MIRANDA	It would become me	
	As well as it does you, and I should do it	
	With much more ease; for my good will is to it,	30
	And yours it is against.	
PROSPERO	Poor worm, thou art	
	infected.	
	This visitation shows it.	
MIRANDA	You look wearily.	
FERDINAND	No, noble mistress, 'tis fresh morning with me	
	When you are by at night. I do beseech you –	
	Chiefly that I might set it in my prayers –	35
	What is your name?	
MIRANDA	Miranda – O my father,	
	I have broke your hest to say so.	
FERDINAND	Admired	
	Miranda,	
	Indeed the top of admiration, worth	
	What's dearest to the world. Full many a lady	
	I have eyed with best regard, and many a time	40
	The harmony of their tongues hath into bondage	
	Brought my too diligent ear. For several virtues	
	Have I lik'd several women, never any	
	With so full soul, but some defect in her	
	Did quarrel with the noblest grace she owed,	45
	And put it to the foil. But you, O you,	
	So perfect and so peerless, are created	

Miranda tells Ferdinand that she has only seen her own face
– no other women and no men except himself and Prospero.
He tells her he is a prince. They agree that they love one
another. Prospero, still looking on, blesses them.

48 **Of every creature's best**: of every human being's best
features
52 **How features are abroad**: what men and women look like
elsewhere, in the wider world
53 **skilless**: ignorant
modesty: virginity
54 **The jewel in my dower**: the most precious quality I have to
offer in marriage
58 **precepts**: commands
59 **condition**: status, rank
61 **I would not so**: I wish this were not the case
62 **suffer**: allow
63 **flesh-fly**: the fly which lays eggs (developing later into
maggots) on dead flesh
blow: lay its eggs on
69 **kind event**: a happy outcome
70 **hollowly**: without substance, falsely
70–71 **invert…mischief**: overturn whatever good things are
meant for me, and turn them into misfortune
72 **what**: whatever
74 **Fair encounter**: a happy meeting
75 **rare**: special
76 **that which breeds**: the love which is growing

Of every creature's best.

MIRANDA   I do not know
One of my sex; no woman's face remember,
Save, from my glass, mine one. Nor have I seen   50
More that I may call men than you good friend,
And my dear father. How features are abroad,
I am skilless of; but by my modesty,
The jewel in my dower, I would not wish
Any companion in the world but you.   55
Nor can imagination form a shape,
Besides yourself, to like of. But I prattle
Something too wildly, and my father's precepts
I therein do forget.

FERDINAND   I am, in my condition,
A prince, Miranda; I do think, a king –   60
I would not so – and would no more endure
This wooden slavery than to suffer
The flesh-fly blow my mouth. Hear my soul speak.
The very instant that I saw you, did
My heart fly to your service; there resides,   65
To make me slave to it; and for your sake
Am I this patient log-man.

MIRANDA   Do you love me?

FERDINAND O heaven, O earth, bear witness to this sound,
And crown what I profess with kind event
If I speak true. If hollowly, invert   70
What best is boded me to mischief. I
Beyond all limit of what else i' th' world
Do love, prize, honour you.

MIRANDA   I am a fool
To weep at what I am glad of.

PROSPERO   Fair encounter
Of two most rare affections. Heavens rain grace   75
On that which breeds between 'em.

FERDINAND   Wherefore

Miranda, although wishing to appear modest, cannot hide
her desires and her delight at the thought of marrying
Ferdinand. They promise marriage. Prospero is pleased, but
leaves, as he still has some magical business to attend to.

77–78 **At mine...to give**: the conventional mention of her
unworthiness is followed by 'offer' and 'desire to give' with
strong sexual overtones
79 **to want**: if I cannot have it
trifling: foolish pretence. Miranda has somehow (from
books?) acquired some of the coy conversation expected of
lovers, but in line 81 she calls on her natural directness to
assert itself
84 **maid**: virgin, but still devoted to him as a maid, meaning
'servant', might be. A wife would be his 'fellow', his equal
89 **As bondage...freedom**: as a slave desires freedom
91 **A thousand thousand**: 'farewells'
93 **Who...withal**: they did not expect this, so their delight is
greater than mine – I arranged it!
96 **appertaining**: relevant to this

Caliban, Stephano and Trinculo are still drinking steadily
from the barrel, though Trinculo has presumably suggested
water instead. Caliban is still in his role of 'servant-monster'.

1 **when the butt is out**: when the barrel is empty
2–3 **bear up, and board 'em**: a phrase taken from sea battles
where another ship is to be attacked and boarded. Here
'drink up'

weep you?

MIRANDA   At mine unworthiness, that dare not offer
What I desire to give, and much less take
What I shall die to want. But this is trifling,
And all the more it seeks to hide itself,   80
The bigger bulk it shows. Hence bashful cunning,
And prompt me plain and holy innocence.
I am your wife, if you will marry me;
If not, I'll die your maid. To be your fellow
You may deny me, but I'll be your servant   85
Whether you will or no.

FERDINAND   My mistress, dearest,
And I thus humble ever.

MIRANDA   My husband then?

FERDINAND   Ay, with a heart as willing
As bondage e'er of freedom. Here's my hand.

MIRANDA   And mine, with my heart in 't. And now farewell 90
Till half an hour hence.

FERDINAND   A thousand thousand.
                    [*Exeunt* FERDINAND *and* MIRANDA *severally*

PROSPERO   So glad of this as they I cannot be,
Who are surprised withal; but my rejoicing
At nothing can be more. I'll to my book,
For yet ere supper-time must I perform   95
Much business appertaining.   [*Exit*

Scene 2

The island

Enter CALIBAN, STEPHANO, *and* TRINCULO

STEPHANO   Tell not me; when the butt is out, we will drink
water, not a drop before; therefore bear up, and
board 'em. Servant-monster, drink to me.

The two men talk drunkenly. Caliban, unused to drink, is almost speechless, but still servile towards Stephano, though not Trinculo, who mocks him.

4 **folly**: absurdity
6 **brained like us**: i.e. as brainless as we are
9 **set**: fixed, staring drunkenly
14 **five and thirty leagues**: a league was not of fixed length but he is claiming a swim of about 100 miles
16 **standard**: standard-bearer (flag bearer), ensign in the army; standard was also a stand-pipe or conduit for a public water supply; a standard is also a fruit or flowering tree which stands clear of supports or wires, unlike a cordon or espalier
17 **list**: choose, or lean
   he's no standard: he cannot stand (a punning reference)
18 **run**: run from the enemy (if the troops could no longer see the standard (flag), to which they could rally, then the battle might well be lost). Using the second meaning of standard (line 16) 'run' can also be a pun on pass water, urinate
19 **go**: walk
   lie: lie down, recline, or tell lies
25 **in case**: in a fit state i.e. drunk and therefore brave enough
26 **justle**: jostle
   deboshed: debauched
33 **a natural**: an idiot, but of course a monster is considered 'unnatural'
36 **the next tree**: the next tree shall be your gallows

> • *Do Stephano and Trinculo help us to understand the attitudes to Caliban of other characters in the play?*

TRINCULO	Servant-monster? The folly of this island. They say there's but five upon this isle; we are three of 5 them; if th' other two be brained like us, the state totters.
STEPHANO	Drink servant-monster when I bid thee. Thy eyes are almost set in thy head.
TRINCULO	Where should they be set else? He were a brave 10 monster indeed if they were set in his tail.
STEPHANO	My man-monster hath drowned his tongue in sack. For my part the sea cannot drown me; I swam, ere I could recover the shore, five and thirty leagues off and on. By this light thou shalt be my lieutenant, 15 monster, or my standard.
TRINCULO	Your lieutenant if you list, he's no standard.
STEPHANO	We'll not run Monsieur Monster.
TRINCULO	Nor go neither. But you'll lie like dogs, and yet say nothing neither. 20
STEPHANO	Moon-calf, speak once in thy life, if thou beest a good moon-calf.
CALIBAN	How does thy honour? Let me lick thy shoe. I'll not serve him, he is not valiant.
TRINCULO	Thou liest most ignorant monster, I am in case 25 to justle a constable. Why, thou deboshed fish thou, was there ever man a coward that hath drunk so much sack as I today? Wilt thou tell a monstrous lie, being but half a fish, and half a monster?
CALIBAN	Lo, how he mocks me. Wilt thou let him my 30 lord?
TRINCULO	'Lord' quoth he? That a monster should be such a natural.
CALIBAN	Lo, lo, again. Bite him to death I prithee.
STEPHANO	Trinculo, keep a good tongue in your head. If 35 you prove a mutineer – the next tree. The poor monster's my subject, and he shall not suffer

While Caliban starts to swear loyalty to Stephano and to explain how Prospero got the island from him by magic, Ariel arrives, unseen, and says that Caliban is telling lies. Caliban and Stephano think Trinculo is speaking. Caliban proposes that Stephano shall kill Prospero while he is sleeping.

40 suit: plea
53 Mum: keep quiet
57 this thing: indicating Trinculo
60 compassed: brought about
65 pied ninny: reference to Trinculo's parti-coloured jester's clothes. 'Ninny' – a fool – is derived from the word 'innocent'
patch: again, derived from the patchwork effect of the jester's clothes, the word is often used for the court fool

- *Why is Caliban so anxious to find fault with Trinculo?*

	indignity.
CALIBAN	I thank my noble lord. Wilt thou be pleased to
	hearken once again to the suit I made to thee? 40
STEPHANO	Marry will I. Kneel and repeat it. I will stand, and
	so shall Trinculo.

Enter ARIEL, *invisible*

CALIBAN	As I told thee before, I am subject to a tyrant, a
	sorcerer, that by his cunning hath cheated me of
	the island. 45
ARIEL	Thou liest.
CALIBAN	Thou liest, thou jesting monkey thou.
	I would my valiant master would destroy thee!
	I do not lie.
STEPHANO	Trinculo, if you trouble him any more in 's tale, 50
	by this hand, I will supplant some of your teeth.
TRINCULO	Why, I said nothing.
STEPHANO	Mum then, and no more. Proceed.
CALIBAN	I say, by sorcery he got this isle;
	From me he got it. If thy greatness will, 55
	Revenge it on him, for I know thou darest,
	But this thing dare not.
STEPHANO	That's most certain.
CALIBAN	Thou shalt be lord of it, and I'll serve thee.
STEPHANO	How now shall this be compassed? Canst thou 60
	bring me to the party?
CALIBAN	Yea, yea my lord, I'll yield him thee asleep,
	Where thou mayst knock a nail into his head.
ARIEL	Thou liest, thou canst not.
CALIBAN	What a pied ninny's this. Thou scurvy patch! 65
	I do beseech thy greatness, give him blows,
	And take his bottle from him. When that's gone,
	He shall drink nought but brine, for I'll not show
	him

Stephano, believing that Trinculo is interrupting Caliban, and calling him a liar, beats him. Caliban continues with the proposal to kill Prospero, and insists they burn his books, which he realises is where Prospero's power lies.

69 **freshes**: springs of fresh water

72–73 **stockfish**: dried cod or hake which needed to be softened by pounding before it was cooked

78 **give me...time**: tell me I'm lying once again

80 **pox**: a curse, a plague. Pox was any feared and disfiguring disease, from the plague to syphilis

81 **murrain**: a plague affecting cattle, used as a mild curse

84–85 **Prithee...farther off**: said to Trinculo, who is mistakenly thought to be calling Caliban a liar and interrupting his story. Some editors claim it is said to Caliban on account of his smell, but this seems unlikely

91 **paunch...stake**: stab him in the gut. To paunch an animal which had been hunted and killed was to empty out the guts

92 **wezand**: wind-pipe

94 **sot**: fool

97 **utensils**: either tools of his sorcery or just household objects. Both should be almost equally puzzling to Caliban

98 **deck**: furnish

99 **And...is**: and what we must also consider carefully

> • *Caliban has obviously dwelt long and lovingly on ways to kill Prospero. Why hasn't he done it?*

	Where the quick freshes are.	
STEPHANO	Trinculo, run into no further danger. Interrupt	70
	the monster one word further, and by this hand,	
	I'll turn my mercy out o' doors, and make a stock-	
	fish of thee.	
TRINCULO	Why, what did I? I did nothing. I'll go farther off.	
STEPHANO	Didst thou not say he lied?	75
ARIEL	Thou liest.	
STEPHANO	Do I so? Take thou that. [*Beats* TRINCULO	
	As you like this, give me the lie another time.	
TRINCULO	I did not give the lie. Out o' your wits and hearing	
	too? A pox o' your bottle, this can sack and	80
	drinking do. A murrain on your monster, and the	
	devil take your fingers!	
CALIBAN	Ha, ha, ha!	
STEPHANO	Now, forward with your tale. Prithee stand farther	
	off.	85
CALIBAN	Beat him enough. After a little time	
	I'll beat him too.	
STEPHANO	Stand farther. Come proceed.	
CALIBAN	Why, as I told thee, 'tis a custom with him	
	I' th' afternoon to sleep. There thou mayst brain	
	him,	
	Having first seized his books, or with a log	90
	Batter his skull, or paunch him with a stake,	
	Or cut his wezand with thy knife. Remember	
	First to possess his books; for without them	
	He's but a sot, as I am, nor hath not	
	One spirit to command. They all do hate him	95
	As rootedly as I. Burn but his books.	
	He has brave utensils – for so he calls them –	
	Which, when he has a house, he'll deck withal.	
	And that most deeply to consider is	
	The beauty of his daughter. He himself	100

Caliban has no difficulty in persuading Stephano that
Miranda will be a suitable queen for him. Fired by this
thought, Stephano agrees to the murder plot, which Ariel
has overheard. Ariel plays the tune Caliban has asked
Stephano to sing.

101 **a nonpareil**: a woman whose beauty cannot be equalled
102 **dam**: mother
104 **brave**: attractive, beautiful
105 **She will...I warrant**: I guarantee she will be a most fitting
partner for you
106 **And bring...brood**: and bear good-looking children for
you
109 **viceroys**: a viceroy has the king's authority to act for him,
sometimes as governor of a province or country
110 **the plot**: the set-up I propose
118 **jocund**: light-hearted, joyful
troll the catch: sing the round
119 **but while-ere**: just a short while ago
120 **I will...reason**: I'll do anything within reason
122 **Flout**: mock, jeer at, insult
scout: sneer at
124 **Thought is free**: a proverbial phrase, popular with people
who feel themselves oppressed
127–128 **the picture of Nobody**: Ariel is invisible so Trinculo
refers to a contemporary, punning depiction of a man with
'no body' with head, arms and legs attached to nothing

- *Who seems to be in control here? How can you tell?*

	Calls her a nonpareil. I never saw a woman,	
	But only Sycorax my dam and she;	
	But she as far surpasseth Sycorax	
	As great'st does least.	
STEPHANO	Is it so brave a lass?	
CALIBAN	Ay lord. She will become thy bed, I warrant,	105
	And bring thee forth brave brood.	
STEPHANO	Monster, I will kill this man. His daughter and I	
	will be king and queen – save our graces! – and	
	Trinculo and thyself shall be viceroys. Dost thou	
	like the plot, Trinculo?	110
TRINCULO	Excellent.	
STEPHANO	Give me thy hand, I am sorry I beat thee. But while	
	thou livest, keep a good tongue in thy head.	
CALIBAN	Within this half hour will he be asleep.	
	Wilt thou destroy him then?	
STEPHANO	Ay on mine	
	honour.	115
ARIEL	This will I tell my master.	
CALIBAN	Thou mak'st me merry. I am full of pleasure;	
	Let us be jocund. Will you troll the catch	
	You taught me but while-ere?	
STEPHANO	At thy request monster, I will do reason, any	
	reason.	120
	Come on, Trinculo, let us sing. [*Sings*	
	Flout 'em and scout 'em	
	And scout 'em and flout 'em;	
	Thought is free.	
CALIBAN	That's not the tune.	125
	[ARIEL *plays the tune on a tabor and pipe*	
STEPHANO	What is this same?	
TRINCULO	This is the tune of our catch, played by the picture	
	of Nobody.	
STEPHANO	If thou beest a man, show thyself in thy likeness; if	

114

Caliban, Stephano and Trinculo are puzzled by the sound of music they cannot trace, and Caliban explains that there are often unaccountable and beautiful sounds on the island. They follow the music away, still with the intention of killing Prospero.

130 **take 't as thou list**: take it as you please
132 **He...debts**: a proverb
137 **sweet airs**: musical sounds, or, possibly, scents
138 **twangling**: a light and continuous jingling sound
144 **I cried**: I called out, pleaded
145 **brave**: splendid
146 **my music for nothing**: court musicians would of course have been paid and part of their function was to make the monarch, as patron, seem important. Stephano is impressed at having this attention free on this strange island

> • *What does Caliban's speech on this page tell us about him? Do you think Antonio could speak like this?*

The royal party is still looking for Ferdinand. Gonzalo is exhausted.

1 **By 'r lakin**: by our ladykin – a milder expression than 'by our Lady' (a reference to the mother of Christ)

	thou beest a devil, take 't as thou list.	130
TRINCULO	O forgive me my sins.
STEPHANO	He that dies pays all debts. I defy thee. Mercy upon us!
CALIBAN	Art thou afeard?
STEPHANO	No monster, not I.	135
CALIBAN	Be not afeard, the isle is full of noises,

Sounds and sweet airs, that give delight and hurt
    not.
Sometimes a thousand twangling instruments
Will hum about mine ears; and sometime voices,
That if I then had waked after long sleep,   140
Will make me sleep again; and then in dreaming,
The clouds methought would open, and show
    riches
Ready to drop upon me, that when I waked,
I cried to dream again.

STEPHANO   This will prove a brave kingdom to me, where I 145
shall have my music for nothing.

CALIBAN   When Prospero is destroyed.

STEPHANO   That shall be by and by. I remember the story.

TRINCULO   The sound is going away. Let's follow it, and after
do our work.   150

STEPHANO   Lead monster, we'll follow. I would I could see this
taborer, he lays it on.

TRINCULO   Wilt come? I'll follow, Stephano.   [*Exeunt*

Scene 3

The island
Enter ALONSO, SEBASTIAN, ANTONIO, GONZALO,
ADRIAN, FRANCISCO, *etc.*

GONZALO   By 'r lakin, I can go no farther, sir;

Alonso is also tired and dispirited. He decides there is no longer any point in searching for his son, he must be dead. Antonio and Sebastian, in asides, agree to pursue their murderous plans when the chance comes. Prospero and his spirits prepare a magic banquet for them.

2 **maze**: a winding movement, especially in a dance, also an artificial maze

3 **forthrights and meanders**: straight and winding paths

5 **attached**: arrested, seized; stopped in my tracks

6 **To the...spirits**: so that my spirits are low, I am depressed

7 **put off**: cast away

10 **frustrate**: (an adjective here) vain, pointless

12 **for one repulse**: just because we've failed once

14 **throughly**: thoroughly
[*on the top*: on the Elizabethan stage there was a gallery above and behind the main playing area]

20 **keepers**: guardian angels. The idea was that each Christian soul had a guardian angel to watch over that person's moral and physical safety

21 **A living drollery**: a puppet-show, possibly (here) where the 'puppets' are living people; a caricature

22 **unicorns**: a unicorn was a legendary creature like a horse, but with one long straight horn on its forehead. A preparation made from the horn was believed to be effective against poison

23 **the phoenix' throne**: where the legendary bird, the phoenix, lived. It was believed to have beautiful coloured plumage and to live for five or six hundred years. It always died in a fire, from the ashes of which it rose again, rejuvenated, to repeat the cycle

My old bones ache. Here's a maze trod indeed
Through forthrights and meanders. By your
        patience,
I needs must rest me.

ALONSO   Old lord, I cannot blame
        thee,
Who am myself attached with weariness   5
To the dulling of my spirits. Sit down, and rest.
Even here I will put off my hope, and keep it
No longer for my flatterer. He is drowned
Whom thus we stray to find, and the sea mocks
Our frustrate search on land. Well, let him go.   10

ANTONIO   [*Aside to* SEBASTIAN] I am right glad that he's so
        out of hope.
Do not, for one repulse, forego the purpose
That you resolved t' effect.

SEBASTIAN   [*Aside to* ANTONIO]   The next advantage
Will we take throughly.

ANTONIO   [*Aside to* SEBASTIAN] Let it be tonight;
For, now they are oppressed with travel, they   15
Will not, nor cannot, use such vigilance
As when they are fresh.

Enter PROSPERO *on the top, invisible. Enter several
strange* SHAPES, *bringing in a banquet; they dance
about it with gentle actions of salutation; and,
inviting the* KING, *& c., to eat, they depart*
                        [*Solemn and strange music*

SEBASTIAN   [*Aside to* ANTONIO] I say, tonight. No more.

ALONSO   What harmony is this? My good friends, hark.

GONZALO   Marvellous sweet music.

ALONSO   Give us kind keepers, heavens. What were these? 20

SEBASTIAN   A living drollery. Now I will believe
That there are unicorns; that in Arabia
There is one tree, the phœnix' throne, one phœnix

The royal group stands amazed at the strange creatures they have seen. Gonzalo comments that they seemed better than many humans. Alonso, too, praises them. Sebastian is merely content they they have left the food behind.

25 **want credit**: lack belief
26 **Travellers ne'er did lie**: it was usually impossible to check whether travellers' tales were true or grossly exaggerated
30 **certes**: certainly
33 **human generation**: produced by human beings
34 **Many, nay almost any**: few if any of the human beings Gonzalo has had dealings with have compared favourably with the 'islanders' he has observed
36 **muse**: wonder at
38 **want the use of tongue**: have no speech
39 **dumb discourse**: mime
   Praise in departing: an adaptation of the proverb that praise should be kept to the end of an occasion, in case first impressions changed
41 **viands**: food
   stomachs: stomachs or good appetites
44 **mountaineers**: people living in the mountains
45 **Dew-lapped**: with loose folds of skin at the throat
46 **Wallets**: wattles, fleshy flaps of skin, like those on a turkey's neck

	At this hour reigning there.
ANTONIO	I'll believe both.
	And what does else want credit, come to me, 25
	And I'll be sworn 'tis true. Travellers ne'er did lie.
	Though fools at home condemn 'em.
GONZALO	If in Naples
	I should report this now, would they believe me?
	If I should say, I saw such islanders –
	For certes these are people of the island – 30
	Who though they are of monstrous shape, yet note,
	Their manners are more gentle-kind than of
	Our human generation you shall find
	Many, nay almost any.
PROSPERO	[*Aside*] Honest lord,
	Thou hast said well. For some of you there present 35
	Are worse than devils.
ALONSO	I cannot too much muse
	Such shapes, such gesture, and such sound expressing –
	Although they want the use of tongue – a kind
	Of excellent dumb discourse.
PROSPERO	[*Aside*] Praise in departing.
FRANCISCO	They vanished strangely.
SEBASTIAN	No matter, since 40
	They have left their viands behind; for we have stomachs.
	Will 't please you taste of what is here?
ALONSO	Not I.
GONZALO	Faith sir, you need not fear. When we were boys,
	Who would believe that there were mountaineers
	Dew-lapped like bulls, whose throats had hanging at 'em 45
	Wallets of flesh? Or that there were such men

Alonso decides to eat, at which the banquet vanishes. Ariel, in the guise of a harpy, a malevolent mythical creature with human face and eagle's wings and talons, tells Alonso, Antonio and Sebastian that in madness they will create their own punishment for their crimes. He says their swords are of no use to them and reminds them of what they did to Prospero and Miranda.

47 **Whose heads...breasts**: people with their head at the level of their chest, not on their shoulders

48 **putter-out of five for one**: a reference to an early kind of travel insurance or investment, where the traveller, often going into unknown dangers, deposited a sum of money to be repaid five-fold on his return, which would help pay his expenses, or be kept by the 'insurer' if he failed to come back

50 **my last**: my last meal
[*harpy*: 'a fabulous monster, rapacious and filthy, having a woman's face and body and bird's wings and claws and supposed to act as a minister of divine vengeance' (*OED* definition)
quaint device: some stage special effect]

53–55 **whom Destiny, That...in 't**: whom Providence, or Fate, which has this lower world for the working out of its intentions

55 **never-surfeited sea**: the sea has not refused to drown them because it has had enough corpses (it never has enough) but because their crimes have made them unpalatable. As they are unfit to live among men, they have been cast up on an uninhabited island

59 **such-like valour**: a false courage induced by fear, anger and madness

60 **proper**: own

61–65 **the elements...plume**: the elements which have come together to make your sword (metal, tempered by fire) might just as well try to wound the winds or stab the waters which will always close together again, as try to destroy the smallest part of one of my feathers

65 **fellow ministers**: other spirits may be attending Ariel in his fateful speech

66 **Are like invulnerable**: like me cannot be injured

67 **too massy**: too solid, too heavy. Prospero has laid a kind of paralysis on them

71 **requit**: avenged the deed

74 **Incensed**: stirred up, enraged

Whose heads stood in their breasts? Which now we
   find
Each putter-out of five for one will bring us
Good warrant of.

ALONSO   I will stand to, and feed,
Although my last: no matter, since I feel   50
The best is past. Brother, my lord the Duke,
Stand to, and do as we.

Thunder and lightning. Enter ARIEL, *like a harpy;*
claps his wings upon the table; and, with a quaint
device, the banquet vanishes

ARIEL   You are three men of sin, whom Destiny,
That hath to instrument this lower world
And what is in 't, the never-surfeited sea   55
Hath caused to belch up you, and on this island
Where man doth not inhabit, you 'mongst men
Being most unfit to live. I have made you mad;
And even with such-like valour men hang, and
   drown
Their proper selves.   [*They draw swords*
                     You fools, I and my fellows 60
Are ministers of Fate: the elements,
Of whom your swords are tempered, may as well
Wound the loud winds, or with bemocked-at stabs
Kill the still-closing waters, as diminish
One dowle that's in my plume. My fellow-
   ministers   65
Are like invulnerable. If you could hurt,
Your swords are now too massy for your strengths,
And will not be uplifted. But remember –
For that's my business to you – that you three
From Milan did supplant good Prospero;   70
Exposed unto the sea, which hath requit it,
Him and his innocent child. For which foul deed
The powers, delaying, not forgetting, have
Incensed the seas and shores, yea, all the creatures,

Ariel, as harpy, goes on to tell Alonso that his son has been taken from him, and he will continue in slow, inexorable punishment. The 'shapes' remove the banqueting table. Prospero praises Ariel and congratulates himself. Alonso goes to seek his dead son and his own death.

77 **Lingering perdition**: slow, ongoing destruction

77–78 **death Can be at once**: sudden death can be

79–82 **whose wraths...life ensuing**: there is no alternative but true repentance and blameless life ever afterwards, to guard you from the anger of those powers (in line 73) which otherwise, in this desolate island, will fall upon your heads [*mocks and mows*: jeers and grimaces]

84 **devouring**: in classical literature the harpies snatched up the food in their claws and greedily ate it, or so dirtied it that it was useless

85 **bated**: left out

86 **So**: in just the same way
with good life: the convincing naturalness

87 **observation strange:** and wonderful attention (to my instructions)
meaner ministers: lesser spirits

88 **Their several kinds have done**: have played out the various roles best suited to them

89–90 **knit up...distractions**: entangled in their own madness

95 **strange stare**: gazing in this horrified way

96 **of it**: of my wicked crime

98 **organ-pipe**: in the reverberations of the thunder Alonso seems to hear Prospero's name, just as words might almost be lost in a deep organ note

99 **It did bass my trespass**: it provided the bass accompaniment to my offence (with pun on 'bass'/'base')

101 **plummet**: the lead weight on a rope used by sailors for sounding and finding the depth of water

> • *What is it that makes Alonso start to feel guilt and remorse and to suspect divine vengence in the loss of his son?*

Against your peace. Thee of thy son, Alonso,   75
They have bereft; and do pronounce by me
Lingering perdition – worse than any death
Can be at once – shall step by step attend
You, and your ways; whose wraths to guard you
        from –
Which here, in this most desolate isle, else falls   80
Upon your heads – is nothing but heart's sorrow
And a clear life ensuing.

He vanishes in thunder; then, to soft music, enter the
SHAPES *again and dance, with mocks and mows, and*
carrying out the table

PROSPERO   Bravely the figure of this harpy hast thou
Performed, my Ariel; a grace it had, devouring.
Of my instruction hast thou nothing bated   85
In what thou hadst to say. So with good life
And observation strange, my meaner ministers
Their several kinds have done. My high charms
        work,
And these mine enemies are all knit up
In their distractions. They now are in my power,   90
And in these fits I leave them, while I visit
Young Ferdinand, whom they suppose is drowned,
And his, and mine loved darling.   [*Exit*

GONZALO   I' the name of something holy, sir, why stand you
In this strange stare?

ALONSO   O, it is monstrous,
        monstrous.   95
Methought the billows spoke, and told me of it;
The winds did sing it to me; and the thunder,
That deep and dreadful organ-pipe, pronounced
The name of Prosper. It did bass my trespass.
Therefore my son i' th' ooze is bedded; and   100
I'll seek him deeper than e'er plummet sounded,
And with him there lie mudded.   [*Exit*

Sebastian will try to fight the apparitions and Antonio goes with him. Gonzalo has not heard what Alonso has heard, and merely assumes that guilt is at last working in all three men. He fears they will do something rash and sends the younger men after them.

102 **But...a time**: if I can fight just one fiend at a time, I'll fight hundreds of them

103 **thy second**: support, as in a duel or boxing match

105 **poison...great time after**: a poison believed to be able to work rather like a time-bomb, a long time after it was administered, and here compared with guilt and possibly remorse

107 **That are...joints**: who have younger legs

108 **ecstasy**: madness

SEBASTIAN   But one fiend at
          a time,
          I'll fight their legions o'er.

ANTONIO   I'll be thy second.
                    [*Exeunt* SEBASTIAN *and* ANTONIO

GONZALO   All three of them are desperate. Their great guilt,
          Like poison given to work a great time after,   105
          Now 'gins to bite the spirits. I do beseech you,
          That are of suppler joints, follow them swiftly,
          And hinder them from what this ecstasy
          May now provoke them to.

ADRIAN   Follow, I pray you.
                                            [*Exeunt*

ACTIVITIES

Keeping track

Scene 1

1 What is it, according to Ferdinand, that makes his hard labour of shifting logs tolerable?
2 What does Miranda offer to do for him?
3 Why is Prospero looking on, unseen?
4 What does Ferdinand mean when he tells Miranda he wishes he were not a king?
5 Is Prospero pleased at what he has seen and overheard?

Scene 2

1 Why is Caliban's loyalty to Stephano and not Trinculo?
2 How does Stephano respond to being treated as a leader of men?
3 How many ways of killing Prospero does Caliban put forward?
4 Which of Caliban's suggestions about the island seems finally to make Stephano decide on action?
5 What exactly is the plot that Ariel will report to Prospero?

Scene 3

1 What conclusion has Alonso reluctantly come to?
2 What plot is being hatched now against Alonso and Gonzalo?
3 Prospero approves of what Gonzalo says about human beings. What does Prospero have in mind?
4 What are Alonso's intentions when he leaves the others?
5 What do Sebastian and Antonio want to do?

Discussion

Scene 1

If the match between the son and daughter of the royal houses of Naples and Milan had been arranged normally, in Italy, there would have been certain formalities.

- The parents would have agreed that it was a suitable match – especially from the political point of view. What are the reasons for and against this match? Assuming they would all eventually return to Italy, what implications might this match have for Alonso and Antonio?

- The young couple would have had chaperoned meetings. What takes the place of this on the island? Who benefits from this arrangement?
- If either of the young people were in love with someone other than their parents' choice, there would probably have been implacable opposition. Does this feature in this case? What effect would you expect strong disapproval from one or both parents to have on the young lovers?

In *The Tempest* Prospero has engineered the arrival on the island of Ferdinand and his meeting with Miranda.

- What train of thought makes him suddenly turn on Ferdinand when things seem to be going so well?
- Why does Prospero set Ferdinand the same task that Caliban usually has to undertake?
- It is this menial task which prompts Ferdinand to tell Miranda what rank he holds, and by implication what he offers her. What does she have to offer him? Judging by her responses to this situation, how well do you think Prospero, a single parent, has brought up his daughter?

Scene 2

1 What are the main effects of copious wine on Caliban? Why does he choose Stephano rather than Trinculo to raise to the status of master and lord?

2 What does Caliban know about Prospero's source of power that can mean success for Stephano's plans?

3 In lines 100–104 we are made aware that living on a virtually uninhabited island has deprived Caliban and Miranda in the same way. What have they both lacked?

4 Lines 104–115 complete our knowledge of what Stephano plans for the island. What are these additional ingredients? How do you think Caliban will feature in their common future?

5 Caliban's speech (lines 136–144) adds a completely unexpected dimension to this scene and to what we know of him so far. Read the lines closely and then say what you feel about them.

Scene 3

1 Is the murderous conspiracy still part of Antonio's and Sebastian's plans? What stopped their efforts last time, and what does the mention of it now seem to produce?

2 How is the group 'softened up' to hear Ariel's/Prospero's accusations and sentence? What do we learn about Sebastian that has not been mentioned so far (lines 68–72)?

3 What role does Gonzalo continue to play? Is he just 'all words'?

Drama

1 Alonso, Antonio and Sebastian return to Naples and a rumour starts
that they have had a strange and unnerving experience on Prospero's
island. They agree to give interviews to three publications, in the
privacy of their apartments. Will they tell the whole truth...?

- In groups of three or four, one interviewee and three interviewers,
  choose which of the three 'royals' you wish to be, and which journal
  you represent. Possible publications with an interest in the subject
  might be: Royal Lives; The Journal for Psychical Research; The
  Magic Circular; Women's World; The Armourers' Manual;
  Explorers' Argosy ... or whatever you choose.
- Carry out the interviews.

2 As yourselves, 'hotseat' Ariel (see HOTSEATING page 196). Ask
anything and everything you'd like to know. For example:

- What is it like to be a spirit?
- What are you actually made of?
- Where did you learn your acting and make-up skills?
- You seem to have a good time, what difference would freedom make?
- What do you think of Prospero?
- How do you get on with Caliban?

Close study

Scene 1

Lines 1–35

1 Do you consider, as Ferdinand does (line 9) that Prospero is
'composed of harshness'? Give evidence to support your answer.
2 Why must Prospero find out the progress of the love affair in this way?
He was the one who orchestrated it. What might the dramatic
necessity be here?
3 Which two remarks of Miranda's in her first speech (lines 15–21)
show vividly the strength of her feelings?
4 What does *'he's safe'* (line 21) suggest about her present relationship
with her father?
5 How do Miranda and Ferdinand 'prove' their love (lines 23–31) to
Prospero's satisfaction?

Lines 37–91

1 Ferdinand, to prove his statement that Miranda is *'the top of
admiration'* (line 38) has to denigrate his earlier flirtations. How does
Miranda reply? What adjectives would you use to describe her answer
(lines 48–59)?
2 Next Ferdinand has to establish his rank and his worthiness. How

would this differ from his usual conversation with women at court? Is Miranda impressed? What four words does she find to bring him back to the central issue?

3 In lines 68–71 Ferdinand swears a solemn oath, but does not propose marriage. This puts Miranda in an awkward position. In lines 78–82 what are the steps in Miranda's 'thinking'? How does she know about *'bashful cunning'*? What qualities in her, shown all through this scene, enable her to propose at last to Ferdinand?

Scene 2

Lines 1–20

1 How many times does Shakespeare remind us in the first three lines that this is another drunken scene? What further references can you find in these twenty lines to liquid and its effects?

2 Is Stephano telling the truth about the way he reached shore?

Lines 21–86

1 When three people are alone together two will usually take sides against the third. How is this managed here? What makes it surprising?

2 Ariel's later intervention is heralded several times before his entrance. Which lines carry the key word?

3 Caliban has shown himself willing to be servile. In what other ways is history repeating itself? Use short quotations to prove your points.

4 What has Ariel observed about the situation? How does he take advantage of it? How important is the timing of what he says?

Lines 87–110

1 If Caliban's assertions in lines 92–98 are correct, has Prospero changed much from his Milan days? What kind of future would he have if he abandoned his books?

2 What does this plot against Prospero inevitably remind us of? Was Prospero merely being paranoid when he accused Ferdinand of being a spy? What part has Miranda twice been cast in, by men with designs on the island?

Lines 136–144

We do not expect a speech like this from Caliban. The word 'curse' (on him and from him) echoes in our ears. How does Shakespeare move us by this speech? From *'Be not afeard'* to *'I cried'* he is a different person. Read it aloud and then decide what qualities in the content and the words make him seem more human.

Scene 3

Lines 7–20

1 Prospero has brought these people to a state of physical and emotional exhaustion. Find the three phrases (in lines 7–10) in which Alonso abandons his son.

2 The stage direction *'Prospero, on the top, invisible'* seems to encapsulate the action of the play. How could you stage the play to produce this effect? What sounds or music would you choose to accompany the 'shapes', the 'spirits' and the paralysing magic elsewhere in the play?

Lines 53–82

1 We have come by stages to the confrontation, but again Ariel is Prospero's mouthpiece. What advantages or disadvantages does this have for the character of Prospero, and for the drama?

2 The speech is blunt. Find examples of words and phrases not normally used when speaking to a king.

3 Prospero works through magic, but what references to religion do you find here, both at the beginning and end of the speech?

4 What might be the philosophy behind the fact that swords never seem to work?

Key speeches

In the central act of a five-act drama, all the strands started in Acts 1 and 2 need to be kept in play. In Act 3 the love story seems to have been brought to a satisfactory state but the two other plots lead the action on.

1 **Scene 2 lines 88–104**
Consider the differences and similarities between Antonio's original plot against Prospero and this one of Caliban's. Fill in the second line from your reading of the play.
- Prospero's studies helped Antonio's plans
- Prospero's books ....
- Antonio was afraid to kill Prospero outright
  Caliban ....
- Antonio did not hate Prospero, he was ambitious and greedy
  Caliban ....
- Antonio took from Prospero
  Prospero took ....
- Antonio had a king to help his conspiracy
  Caliban has ....
- If Antonio had done nothing he might never have had the title of duke
  If Caliban left plotting well alone he would ....
- When Antonio made his plot he already had a lot of good things
  When Caliban made his ....

In one respect at least, both Caliban and Miranda are innocents. Find and quote Miranda's lines which echo those of Caliban in lines 101–104.

It is unusual that the comic scenes in Shakespeare's plays also contain villainy which might lead to murder. This speech of Caliban's could be played for comedy – the piling up of murderous ideas almost invites this, but it could be done with full evil intent. How would you direct it, or act it?

2 **Scene 3 lines 53–82**

The use of the harpy invokes mythological references to terrifying and implacable punishment by the gods. Even a king who had offended might be deprived of food in this way, because it was either fouled by these creatures or continually snatched away and devoured.

In this speech Prospero is effectively victim, judge and potential executioner; possibly also stern deity, holding out hope of a new life.

Make notes for your guidance on the various aspects of this speech:

A Lines 53–59 on the general accusation that they have sinned. Note:
   - the religious element in lines 53 and 54
   - the strong imagery and what it is based on
   - how Ariel attacks their pride
   - the threat
B Lines 60–68 on their impotence
   - the imagery
   - the alliteration (end line 62-63) and what effect it has
   - the same for the assonance in line 64
C Lines 68–76 on the indictment
   - the suggestion that all nature has been raised against them
   - confirmation of the punishment Alonso already expects
D Lines 76–82 on the sentence and the hope of grace
   - what the sentence is
   - what the only hope is.

Writing

1 Whether you have taken part in one of the interview sessions in Drama or not, write up one of the interviews suggested there as an article in a style you choose for any of the publications suggested, or an appropriate publication of your choice, real or imaginary.
2 In Acts 2 and 3 Prospero does not play an active part on stage. He is in control, but in the way that a puppet master might be – above, behind, beyond. How does this affect the way we perceive him – both as a person and as the central character of the play?
3 Compare and contrast what we know of Claribel's engagement and marriage (Act 2 scene 1 lines 118–31) and that which Prospero is organising for Miranda. Consider, for example:
   - parental attitudes   • love
   - politics   • obedience.

Prospero tells Ferdinand that his harshness towards him was only to test the strength of his love for Miranda. He now gives her to him, warning him not to sleep with her until they are married. Ferdinand gives his promise.

1 **austerely**: (here) harshly
3 **a third...life**: discussion about what the 'third' constitutes includes: 1. Prospero/Milan/Miranda; 2. Prospero/his wife/Miranda; 3. one third of his life so far which he has spent rearing Miranda. Since he has very recently been reminded of his wife's virtues and possibly of his love for her, in his narrative to Miranda, the second option seems the most likely
5 **tender**: offer
7 **strangely**: wonderfully well
8 **ratify**: confirm
9 **boast her off**: boast about her, praise her to the skies
11 **halt**: limp, follow lamely
12 **Against an oracle**: even if an oracle were to indicate otherwise
14 **Worthily purchased**: deservedly won (because you have suffered for her)
16 **sanctimonious**: holy
18 **aspersion**: sprinkling or scattering (of blessings) and the beginning of a series of words which implies that marriage needs fostering as a garden does: 'grow', 'barren', 'bed', 'weeds'
20 **bestrew**: flowers were commonly spread on the marriage bed
21 **loathly**: loathsome, hateful, disgusting
22 **hate it both**: both hate it
23 **Hymen's lamps**: Hymen, the god of marriage, was commonly depicted with a flaming torch
24 **fair issue**: fine children
25 **the murkiest den**: the most obscure spot
23–31 **As I hope...chained below**: Ferdinand pledges that whatever the temptations of time, place and mood he will not take advantage of Miranda. The pleasure of sleeping with her shall crown their wedding day

Act four

Scene 1

Before PROSPERO's *cell*

Enter PROSPERO, FERDINAND, *and* MIRANDA

PROSPERO   If I have too austerely punished you,
Your compensation makes amends, for I
Have given you here a third of mine own life,
Or that for which I live; who once again
I tender to thy hand. All thy vexations   5
Were but my trials of thy love, and thou
Hast strangely stood the test. Here, afore Heaven
I ratify this my rich gift. O Ferdinand,
Do not smile at me that I boast her off,
For thou shalt find she will outstrip all praise,   10
And make it halt behind her.

FERDINAND   I do believe it
Against an oracle.

PROSPERO   Then, as my gift, and thine own acquisition
Worthily purchased, take my daughter. But
If thou dost break her virgin-knot before   15
All sanctimonious ceremonies may
With full and holy rite be ministered,
No sweet aspersion shall the heavens let fall
To make this contract grow; but barren hate,
Sour-eyed disdain, and discord shall bestrew   20
The union of your bed with weeds so loathly
That you shall hate it both. Therefore take heed.
As Hymen's lamps shall light you.

FERDINAND   As I hope
For quiet days, fair issue, and long life,
With such love as 'tis now, the murkiest den,   25

Prospero trusts Ferdinand's promise that Miranda shall remain a virgin until their wedding night. He congratulates Ariel on his recent performance and orders him, with the other spirits, to put on a show to celebrate the engagement of Ferdinand and Miranda.

26 most opportune place: most convenient place

26–27 the strong'st...can: the strongest temptation which the worst side of us can offer

29 The edge: as in *Hamlet*, the word carries the meaning of 'sexual drive'

30–31 or Phoebus' steeds...chained below: either, the sun-god's horses have fallen lame (so that the day cannot end), or, that night has somehow been imprisoned

35 meaner fellows: lesser spirits

37 the rabble: the whole crowd of them

41 Some vanity of mine art: some show to display my magic skills

42 Presently?: straightaway?

43 with a twink: in the twinkling of an eye

47 mop and mow: 'mock and mow' again

50 conceive: understand

51–52 Do not...the rein: do not tempt each other with too much flirting

53 Be more abstemious: be more sparing, avoid so much togetherness

The most opportune place, the strong'st suggestion
Our worser genius can, shall never melt
Mine honour into lust, to take away
The edge of that day's celebration,
When I shall think or Phœbus' steeds are
    foundered,   30
Or Night kept chained below.

PROSPERO   Fairly spoke.
Sit then, and talk with her, she is thine own.
What Ariel, my industrious servant Ariel!

Enter ARIEL

ARIEL   What would my potent master? Here I am.

PROSPERO   Thou, and thy meaner fellows, your last service   35
Did worthily perform. And I must use you
In such another trick. Go bring the rabble,
O'er whom I give thee power, here to this place.
Incite them to quick motion, for I must
Bestow upon the eyes of this young couple   40
Some vanity of mine art. It is my promise,
And they expect it from me.

ARIEL   Presently?

PROSPERO   Ay, with a twink.

ARIEL   Before you can say, 'come' and 'go',
    And breathe twice, and cry, 'so, so',   45
    Each one tripping on his toe,
    Will be here with mop and mow.
    Do you love me master? No?

PROSPERO   Dearly, my delicate Ariel. Do not approach
Till thou dost hear me call.

ARIEL   Well, I conceive.   50
                              [*Exit*

PROSPERO   Look thou be true. Do not give dalliance
Too much the rein. The strongest oaths are straw
To the fire i' th' blood. Be more abstemious,

Prospero has tried to make sure that Ferdinand behaves himself and now turns his attention to their entertainment. To soft music, Iris, the messenger of the gods, asks Ceres, the goddess of plenty and blessing to come and entertain the queen of the gods, and patroness of marriage, Juno.

54 **Or…vow**: or you can say goodbye to your vow
55–56 **The white cold…liver**: the chill that his vow of chastity has placed on any lust he might have felt. The liver was considered to be the organ governing passion
57 **bring a corollary**: bring more spirits than you need
58 **Rather…spirit**: rather than have too few
and pertly: and be lively
59 **No tongue**: no sound of a voice – this was thought to affect the working of magic
60 **leas**: fields
61 **vetches**: plants grown as fodder for farm animals
62 **turfy**: grassy
63 **meads**: meadows
stover: winter feed for cattle; hay made from clover
64 **pioned and twilled brims**: some claim these two words refer to flowers, but 'pioneer' means 'digger' and it is likely that digging would keep the streams unsilted, and the banks would be shored up with pliable woven 'twilled' willow branches
65 **spongy April**: April is famous for its showers, so the ground is soft and spongey
betrims: decorates with flowers
66 **To make…crowns**: to make modest garlands for virtuous girls
broom-groves: broom is a yellow-flowered plant which can grow quite tall and strong. It was believed to encourage success in love affairs
67 **dismissed**: rejected
68 **lass-lorn**: having lost the love of his girl
poll-clipt: trimmed, pruned; 'poll' means 'head' or (here) top
69 **sea-marge**: sea-shore
70 **Where…air**: where you take the air
the queen o' th' sky: Juno was the wife of Jupiter, King of the gods
74 **sport**: entertain her
peacocks: birds sacred to Juno
amain: with all speed
80 **thy blue bow**: Iris appears as a rainbow
81 **bosky acres**: tree-covered, wooded land
unshrubbed down: bare, grassy downland

Or else good night your vow.

FERDINAND   I warrant you, sir,
The white cold virgin snow upon my heart   55
Abates the ardour of my liver.

PROSPERO   Well.
Now come my Ariel, bring a corollary,
Rather than want a spirit. Appear, and pertly.
No tongue. All eyes. Be silent.   [*Soft music*

Enter IRIS

IRIS   Ceres, most bounteous lady, thy rich leas   60
Of wheat, rye, barley, vetches, oats, and pease;
Thy turfy mountains, where live nibbling sheep,
And flat meads thatched with stover, them to keep;
Thy banks with pioned and twilled brims,
Which spongy April at thy hest betrims,   65
To make cold nymphs chaste crowns; and thy
          broom-groves,
Whose shadow the dismissed bachelor loves,
Being lass-lorn; thy poll-clipt vineyard;
And thy sea-marge, sterile and rocky-hard,
Where thou thyself dost air; – the queen o' th'
          sky,   70
Whose watery arch and messenger am I,
Bids thee leave these, and with her sovereign grace,
                              [JUNO *descends*
Here on this grass-plot, in this very place,
To come and sport. Her peacocks fly amain.
Approach, rich Ceres, her to entertain.   75

Enter CERES

CERES   Hail, many-coloured messenger, that ne'er
Dost disobey the wife of Jupiter;
Who with thy saffron wings upon my flowers
Diffusest honey-drops, refreshing showers,
And with each end of thy blue bow dost crown   80
My bosky acres and my unshrubbed down,

Iris explains to Ceres that she has been asked to attend the betrothal of two lovers. Ceres anxiously asks whether Venus and her son Cupid will be present as she has sworn not to meet them since they plotted to send her daughter Prosperpine to live with the King of the Underworld. Iris reassures her and says they had conspired to make Ferdinand break his vow to Prospero. Juno arrives to pronounce a blessing.

82 **scarf**: ornament
85 **donation**: gift
   estate: bestow
87 **Venus**: the goddess of love
89 **dusky Dis**: dark King of the Underworld, a place where there is no natural light
90 **blind boy**: Cupid
   scandalled: touched by scandal, disgraceful
91 **forsworn**: sworn to reject
   society: company
92 **her deity**: a jokey invention to parallel 'her ladyship' – 'her goddess-ship'
93 **Cutting the clouds**: as a ship 'cuts through' the waves
   Paphos: a place in Cyprus, sacred to Venus
94 **Dove-drawn**: in their chariot, drawn by doves
95 **wanton**: capricious
96 **bed-right**: sleeping together
97 **Till Hymen's...lighted**: i.e. until the wedding ceremony has been performed
98 **Mars's hot minion**: Mars's mistress (Venus), full of desire. She was actually the wife of Vulcan, but often unfaithful to him
99 **waspish-headed**: he is peevish and petulant, and aims his arrows which sting
101 **a boy right out**: just a boy
101–102 **Highest...Juno comes**: great Juno, most stately queen, approaches
102 **gait**: manner, bearing
103 **bounteous**: generous
107 **Long...increasing**: long life and children

Rich scarf to my proud earth. Why hath thy queen
Summoned me hither, to this short-grassed green?

IRIS A contract of true love to celebrate,
And some donation freely to estate   85
On the blest lovers.

CERES   Tell me heavenly bow,
If Venus or her son, as thou dost know,
Do now attend the queen? Since they did plot
The means that dusky Dis my daughter got,
Her and her blind boy's scandalled company   90
I have forsworn.

IRIS   Of her society
Be not afraid. I met her deity
Cutting the clouds towards Paphos, and her son
Dove-drawn with her. Here thought they to have
      done
Some wanton charm upon this man and maid,   95
Whose vows are, that no bed-right shall be paid
Till Hymen's torch be lighted. But in vain;
Mars's hot minion is returned again;
Her waspish-headed son has broke his arrows,
Swears he will shoot no more, but play with
      sparrows,   100
And be a boy right out.

CERES   Highest queen of state,
Great Juno comes, I know her by her gait.

Enter JUNO

JUNO How does my bounteous sister? Go with me
To bless this twain, that they may prosperous be
And honoured in their issue.   105
                                        [*They sing*

JUNO Honour, riches, marriage-blessing,
Long continuance, and increasing,
Hourly joys be still upon you.
Juno sings her blessings on you.

The celebratory masque continues, with blessings on Ferdinand and Miranda from Juno and Ceres. Ferdinand is impressed with the magical skills of his father-in-law to be. Suddenly Ferdinand, too, pictures himself living on the island for ever.

111 garners: storehouses for corn, granaries

113 with goodly burthen bowing: weighed down with fruit

114–115 Spring…harvest: a wish that spring should follow straight on from autumn, without the interruption of winter

117 so: to such an extent

119 Harmonious charmingly: a comment which combines reference to music and Prospero's magic

119–120 May I be bold…spirits?: may I assume these are spirits

121 their confines: their natural surroundings

123–124 So rare…Paradise: a father to be wondered at and a father who produces wonders. There is a strong possibility expressed by commentators that Shakespeare wrote 'wife' not 'wise'. This would reinforce the feeling that Prospero is God and Ferdinand and Miranda are Adam and Eve in this paradise

124 Sweet: a man could properly address another man as 'sweet', or Prospero may have been thinking Miranda was about to speak and break the spell

128 nymphs: in mythology, semi-divine beings living in rivers, seas, springs, hills, woods, trees, etc
Naiads: river-nymphs
windring: either a misprint for winding or Shakespeare playing successfully with a combination of winding and wandering

129 sedged: sedge is a grass- or rush-like plant growing in or near water. Here it has been woven into garlands
harmless: innocent

130 crisp: with little curling waves

132 temperate: moderate, restrained – a chaste example for Ferdinand and Miranda to follow

134 sicklemen…weary: farm labourers wielding sickles, weary of August because it is the busy harvest-time

CERES	Earth's increase, foison plenty,	110
	Barns and garners never empty,	
	Vines with clustering bunches growing,	
	Plants with goodly burthen bowing.	
	Spring come to you at the farthest	
	In the very end of harvest.	115
	Scarcity and want shall shun you.	
	Ceres' blessing so is on you.	
FERDINAND	This is a most majestic vision, and	
	Harmonious charmingly. May I be bold	
	To think these spirits?	
PROSPERO	Spirits, which by mine	
	art	120
	I have from their confines called to enact	
	My present fancies.	
FERDINAND	Let me live here ever;	
	So rare a wondered father, and a wise	
	Makes this place Paradise.	

[JUNO *and* CERES *whisper, and send* IRIS *on
employment*

PROSPERO	Sweet now, silence.	
	Juno and Ceres whisper seriously;	125
	There's something else to do. Hush, and be mute,	
	Or else our spell is marred.	
IRIS	You nymphs, called Naiads, of the windring brooks,	
	With your sedged crowns and ever-harmless looks,	
	Leave your crisp channels, and on this green	
	land	130
	Answer your summons; Juno does command.	
	Come temperate nymphs, and help to celebrate	
	A contract of true love. Be not too late.	

Enter certain NYMPHS

You sunburnt sicklemen of August weary,
Come hither from the furrow, and be merry.   135
Make holiday. Your rye-straw hats put on,

Towards the end of the dance of the nymphs and harvesters, Prospero gives a start and the dance fades out to the accompaniment of a strange noise. Ferdinand and Miranda are concerned at Prospero's anger but he has just remembered the Caliban conspiracy. Prospero merely explains that the show is over and he has to think.

138 **footing**: dance
142 **avoid**: go
144 **works him**: disturbs him
145 **distempered**: upset
146 **in a moved sort**: in a troubled state, or frame of mind
149 **foretold you**: told you before
151 **baseless fabric...vision**: sights not founded in reality
154 **all which it inherit**: everyone who comes into possession of it in turn
155 **pageant**: the stage and scenes or tableaux presented on the stage
156 **rack**: thin, light cloud or drifting mist or fog
157 **on**: of
158 **rounded**: finished off
159 **my old brain is troubled**: Prospero has temporarily forgotten what Ariel told him of the plot against his life. Not only Prospero but all his carefully laid and orchestrated plans are at risk. He has had a shock. 'My old brain' excuses his odd behaviour and gives him time to himself to plan his next steps.

It is a widely-held view that *The Tempest* marks Shakespeare's retirement as court playwright and lines 148–158 can certainly be read as his leave-taking. The epilogue (page 181) too can be interpreted as a request to his royal patron, James I, to allow him to give up his post
162 **repose**: rest
163 **To still...mind**: to quieten my agitated thoughts

- *What might be the cause of Prospero's sudden lapse of memory?*
- *Why might Ferdinand justly seem so 'dismayed' by this sudden change of mood?*

And these fresh nymphs encounter every one
In country footing.

Enter certain REAPERS, *properly habited: they join
with the* NYMPHS *in a graceful dance; towards the
end whereof* PROSPERO *starts suddenly, and speaks;
after which, to a strange, hollow, and confused noise,
they heavily vanish*

PROSPERO   [*Aside*] I had forgot that foul conspiracy
            Of the beast Caliban and his confederates   140
            Against my life. The minute of their plot
            Is almost come. [*To the* SPIRITS] Well done, avoid.
                No more.

FERDINAND   This is strange. Your father's in some passion
            That works him strongly.

MIRANDA   Never till this day
            Saw I him touched with anger so distempered.   145

PROSPERO   You do look, my son, in a moved sort,
            As if you were dismayed. Be cheerful sir.
            Our revels now are ended. These our actors,
            As I foretold you, were all spirits, and
            Are melted into air, into thin air;   150
            And like the baseless fabric of this vision,
            The cloud-capped towers, the gorgeous palaces,
            The solemn temples, the great globe itself,
            Yea, all which it inherit, shall dissolve,
            And like this insubstantial pageant faded,   155
            Leave not a rack behind. We are such stuff
            As dreams are made on, and our little life
            Is rounded with a sleep. Sir, I am vexed;
            Bear with my weakness; my old brain is troubled.
            Be not disturbed with my infirmity.   160
            If you be pleased, retire into my cell,
            And there repose: a turn or two I'll walk
            To still my beating mind.

When Miranda and Ferdinand have left, Prospero summons Ariel and asks where he left Caliban and the other two. Ariel explains that in their drunken excitement they were eager to carry out their murderous plot. But he led them astray with his music and they followed him through thorns and prickles into a stagnant pond nearby. Ariel is told to fetch some bait to trap them with.

164 **with a thought**: as quick as thought
I thank thee: Prospero thanks them for their good wishes. Again a singular pronoun for the plural 'you'
165 **Thy thoughts...to**: 'cleave to' means 'cling to'. Ariel is saying 'Your thoughts are my command'
167 **presented Ceres**: played Ceres in the masque
170 **varlets**: originally meaning servants, here with the additional sense of 'rogues'
172 **smote**: hit out at
174 **bending**: tending towards, aiming for
176 **unbacked colts**: when it is time for a young horse to be trained for riding (to be 'broken'), it is ideally handled and gentled by its trainer and eventually 'backed', that is allowed to feel by degrees the weight of a human being on its back. 'Unbacked' means 'unbroken' rather than 'never ridden'
177 **Advanced**: raised
178 **So I charmed their ears**: I charmed their ears to such an extent
179 **calf-like...followed**: a calf will follow the lowing sound made by its mother
180 **sharp furzes, pricking goss**: furze and gorse are the same plant, yellow-flowered and fiercely prickly. This is repetition for effect
182 **filthy-mantled**: covered in slime
184 **O'erstunk**: outstank, smelt worse than
my bird: a term of endearment, but he does fly
186 **trumpery**: trash, usually gaudy costumes in productions of this play
187 **stale**: decoy (as in duck shoots), bait
188 **nature**: the inherent character, disposition, of a person with which they are born

FERDINAND ⎫ MIRANDA ⎭	We wish your peace.

[Exeunt

PROSPERO   Come with a thought. I thank thee. Ariel come.

Enter ARIEL

ARIEL   Thy thoughts I cleave to. What's thy
pleasure?

PROSPERO   Spirit,   165
We must prepare to meet with Caliban.

ARIEL   Ay my commander, when I presented Ceres,
I thought to have told thee of it; but I feared
Lest I might anger thee.

PROSPERO   Say again, where didst thou leave these varlets?   170

ARIEL   I told you sir, they were red-hot with drinking;
So full of valour that they smote the air
For breathing in their faces; beat the ground
For kissing of their feet; yet always bending
Towards their project. Then I beat my tabor;   175
At which, like unbacked colts, they pricked their
ears,
Advanced their eyelids, lifted up their noses
As they smelt music. So I charmed their ears
That calf-like they my lowing followed through
Toothed briers, sharp furzes, pricking goss and,
thorns,   180
Which entered their frail shins. At last I left them
I' th' filthy-mantled pool beyond your cell,
There dancing up to th' chins, that the foul lake
O'erstunk their feet.

PROSPERO   This was well done, my bird.
Thy shape invisible retain thou still.   185
The trumpery in my house, go bring it hither,
For stale to catch these thieves.

ARIEL   I go, I go.   *[Exit*

PROSPERO   A devil, a born devil, on whose nature

Prospero now despairs of Caliban, whom he had tried to teach, but who has deeply disappointed him. Ariel hangs the gaudy clothes on the line and he and Prospero stay there, invisible, as Caliban, Stephano and Trinculo come in, most indignant at their treatment. Caliban indicates Prospero's cell.

189 **Nurture**: upbringing, moral education
192 **cankers**: becomes corrupted
193 **on this line**: this could be either a lime tree or a clothes line
194 **the blind mole**: moles are not blind; they have very small eyes but do not need to rely on sight as they live mostly underground. Their hearing is acute and they also use the sensation of vibrations in the soil to alert them to the presence of food or danger
196 **your fairy**: we must assume that Caliban, as they followed the music, had claimed that they were led by a harmless spirit, a 'fairy'
197 **played the Jack**: tricked us – the Jack is the knave, as in a pack of cards
205 **hoodwink this mischance**: make this misfortune harmless. 'Hoodwink' means 'blindfold'
210 **my wetting**: Ariel had led them deep into the filthy pond. (In *A Midsummer Night's Dream*, Puck leads the Athenian workmen a similar dance)
212 **fetch off my bottle**: dredge up my bottle from the pond

> • *The so-called 'nature/nurture' debate is at its most explicit here. Is it 'nature' – the qualities we are born with, the legacy of our genes – or 'nuture' – the care we are given, the quality of our moral education, our whole environment – which determines our personality?*

Nurture can never stick; on whom my pains,
Humanely taken, all, all lost, quite lost;   190
And as with age his body uglier grows,
So his mind cankers. I will plague them all,
Even to roaring.

Enter ARIEL, *loaden with glistering apparel, & c*

Come, hang them on this line.

PROSPERO *and* ARIEL *remain, invisible. Enter*
CALIBAN, STEPHANO, *and* TRINCULO, *all wet*

CALIBAN   Pray you tread softly, that the blind mole may not
Hear a foot fall; we now are near his cell.   195

STEPHANO   Monster, your fairy, which you say is a harmless fairy,
has done little better than played the Jack with us.

TRINCULO   Monster, I do smell all horse-piss, at which my nose
is in great indignation.

STEPHANO   Do you hear, monster? If I should take a   200
displeasure against you, look you –

TRINCULO   Thou wert but a lost monster.

CALIBAN   Good my lord, give me thy favour still.
Be patient, for the prize I'll bring thee to
Shall hoodwink this mischance. Therefore speak
softly.   205
All's hushed as midnight yet.

TRINCULO   Ay, but to lose our bottles in the pool –

STEPHANO   There is not only disgrace and dishonour in that,
monster, but an infinite loss.

TRINCULO   That's more to me than my wetting. Yet this is   210
your harmless fairy, monster.

STEPHANO   I will fetch off my bottle, though I be o'er ears for
my labour.

CALIBAN   Prithee, my king, be quiet. See'st thou here,
This is the mouth o' th' cell. No noise, and
enter.   215

As the three approach Prospero's cell, Stephano and Trinculo catch sight of the clothes and start to quarrel over them. Only Caliban realises it is rubbish and urges them to murder Prospero first. They will not pay attention to his warnings.

216 **Do that good mischief**: (an oxymoron, see GLOSSARY page 225) do an evil deed so that good can come of it

225 **frippery**: secondhand clothes shop

229 **dropsy**: a disease which causes fluid to accumulate in the body tissues

230 **luggage**: something that has to be 'lugged about', and so something that gets in the way

233 **Make us strange stuff**: make strange matter out of us, with a reference to the clothes, as stuff also means material

234 **Mistress line**: Stephano addresses the line, personifying it. He is presumably still quite drunk

235 **under the line**: under the clothes-line. 'Line' is also the equator, so that the jerkin is also south of the equator, having 'crossed the line'

236 **like to lose your hair**: it was believed that people often lost their hair in fevers contracted in the tropics. This may also be a reference to the ceremony of crossing the line, where a ship's passengers on their first crossing might have their heads shaved

237 **bald**: (here) threadbare

238 **by line and level**: with methodical accuracy (the reference is to the sailor's plumb-line and the carpenter's level)
an 't like: if it please

243–244 **pass of pate**: shaft of wit, witty remark. The term comes from a thrust in fencing

244 **lime**: (here) a sticky substance used for trapping birds. Compare the phrase 'he has sticky fingers' meaning he is liable to steal

247 **turned to barnacles**: barnacle was originally, and still is, the name of a type of goose. It was believed that it grew out of the fruit of a tree, or from the tree itself, attached by its bill – or from the small shelled sea creature, also called a barnacle, attached by a long fleshy foot to old wood, the hulls of boats etc. Caliban has considerable experience of, and belief in, the strength of Prospero's powers

248 **With foreheads, villainous low**: low foreheads, allegedly like those of criminals

249 **lay-to your fingers**: set your fingers to work

	Do that good mischief which may make this island
	Thine own for ever, and I, thy Caliban,
	For aye thy foot-licker.
STEPHANO	Give me thy hand. I do begin to have bloody
	thoughts. 220
TRINCULO	O king Stephano, O peer! O worthy Stephano!
	Look what a wardrobe here is for thee.
CALIBAN	Let 't alone, thou fool, it is but trash.
TRINCULO	O, ho, monster, we know what belongs to a
	frippery. O king Stephano! 225
STEPHANO	Put off that gown, Trinculo, by this hand I'll have
	that gown.
TRINCULO	Thy grace shall have it.
CALIBAN	The dropsy drown this fool. What do you mean
	To dote thus on such luggage? Let 't alone, 230
	And do the murder first. If he awake,
	From toe to crown he'll fill our skins with pinches,
	Make us strange stuff.
STEPHANO	Be you quiet, monster. Mistress line, is not this my
	jerkin? Now is the jerkin under the line. Now, 235
	jerkin, you are like to lose your hair, and prove a
	bald jerkin.
TRINCULO	Do, do: we steal by line and level, an 't like your
	grace.
STEPHANO	I thank thee for that jest; here's a garment for 't. 240
	Wit shall not go unrewarded while I am king of this
	country. 'Steal by line and level' is an excellent pass
	of pate; there's another garment for 't.
TRINCULO	Monster, come put some lime upon your fingers,
	and away with the rest. 245
CALIBAN	I will have none on 't. We shall lose our time,
	And all be turned to barnacles, or to apes
	With foreheads, villainous low.
STEPHANO	Monster, lay-to your fingers. Help to bear this

As Stephano and Trinculo load Caliban down with the goods they want to take away, Prospero and Ariel set spirit dogs and a spirit pack of hounds on them. Shouting to the animals, to encourage them, they drive the three away. Prospero orders their punishment and promises Ariel that his service is nearly at an end.

257 charge: order
257–258 grind…convulsions: a reference to the painful cracking sound, one of the effects of rheumatism and arthritis
259 aged cramps: cramps suffered in old age
260 pard or cat o' mountain: leopards do have spots, panthers (usually indicated by the phrase cat o' mountain) do not, but other wild cats are spotted or blotched

away where my hogshead of wine is, or I'll turn 250
you out of my kingdom. Go to, carry this.

TRINCULO   And this.

STEPHANO   Ay, and this.

A noise of hunters heard. Enter divers SPIRITS, *in
shape of dogs and hounds, and hunt them about,*
PROSPERO *and* ARIEL *setting them on*

PROSPERO   Hey, Mountain, hey!

ARIEL   Silver! there it goes, Silver!   255

PROSPERO   Fury, Fury! There, Tyrant, there! Hark! Hark!

[CALIBAN, STEPHANO, *and* TRINCULO *are driven out*

Go charge my goblins that they grind their joints
With dry convulsions, shorten up their sinews
With aged cramps, and more pinch-spotted make
    them
Than pard or cat o' mountain.

ARIEL   Hark, they
            roar.   260

PROSPERO   Let them be hunted soundly. At this hour
Lie at my mercy all mine enemies.
Shortly shall all my labours end, and thou
Shalt have the air at freedom. For a little
Follow, and do me service.   [*Exeunt* 265

ACTIVITIES

Keeping track

1 Why, according to him, did Prospero treat Ferdinand so harshly?
2 Did Ferdinand pass the test?
3 What condition does Prospero make about the engagement?
4 What are the main messages put across in the masque?
5 Why does the masque come to such an abrupt end?
6 What is the effect on Ferdinand of Prospero's sudden change of mood? What has happened earlier in the play to make this particularly worrying for Ferdinand?
7 How had Ariel dealt with Caliban, Stephano and Trinculo?
8 How does Prospero plan to trap them?
9 Which of these three conspirators is the most sensible?
10 What makes Caliban and the others leave suddenly at the end of Act 4?

Discussion

A Lines 1–56
Prospero has returned in his own person to the action.
1 What impression do you have of his feelings towards Miranda?
2 Does Ferdinand sound sincere in his promises?
3 What consequences does Prospero believe sex before marriage will have for Ferdinand and Miranda's married life? Ferdinand's reassurances are very vehement – does this seem to you to make them more credible or less so?

B Lines 60–138
4 The blessing given by each goddess fits her role. What does Juno bestow on them? What are Ceres' wishes for them?
5 Bearing in mind that Prospero has engineered a betrothal between his daughter and the son of his oldest enemy, what other function might these blessings have from the audience's point of view?
6 Why is Ceres so concerned that Venus and Cupid should not be in attendance on Juno (lines 94–97)?
7 The idea of living on the island has meant different things to different people. What does Ferdinand think of it?

C Lines 139–163
8 What must the thought of 'conspiracy' evoke in Prospero's mind?
9 What is Prospero's frame of mind (lines 152–158)?
10 Does Prospero seem to trust Ferdinand's honourable intentions now?

D Lines 171–193

11 What picture does Ariel present of the three conspirators, Stephano, Trinculo and Caliban?

12 Without the operation of magic and Ariel's lively and humorous report of what happened, how might we be viewing the conspirators and anticipating the outcome of the plot?

13 Prospero seems convinced (lines 188–190) that Caliban is, and always has been, incapable of improvement. Have we any evidence to set against this certainty?

Look at these references to the claims of nature and nurture in *The Tempest*:

- Act 1 scene 2 lines 117–119, line 335, lines 344–346 and lines 351–353
  In Act 1 is it purely a conviction that Caliban is 'a devil' who cannot be changed that establishes 'nature' as the culprit? Or is Prospero angry and deeply hurt because of one action by Caliban?
- Act 2 scene 1 lines 269–270
- Act 3 scene 2 lines 136–144
- Act 4 scene 1 lines 140, 188–190
  What do you consider is the trigger for this comment of Prospero's in Act 4? What has happened to affect his feelings at this stage?

14 We have heard Ariel complain about his servitude. Look at the range of his activites so far in the play. Can you find any evidence that he enjoys at least some of these feats and also the praise he receives from Prospero?

- In Act 1 Ariel manages the storm and the shipwreck. He gives us the details in scene 2 lines 195–237. In lines 252–257 Prospero tells us what Ariel's tasks have been.
- He is a skilful musician. In Act 1 scene 2 lines 375–402 his song suggests to Ferdinand that his father is drowned and draws him to where Miranda is.
- Ariel's music plays a role in Act 2 scene 1 at his entry at line 177 and again at line 290. What is the purpose here? How is it important for the plot?
- In Act 3 scene 2 Ariel has three distinct functions – what are they?
- In Act 3 scene 3 Ariel is director of the 'shapes' and dramatic actor as a harpy.
- In Act 4 he presents and acts in the masque.

15 Some critics see in the roles of Caliban and Ariel two opposing sides of Prospero's own nature, both of which have more free play on the island than was ever possible in Milan.

How do you react to this suggestion? If you think there is some truth in it, how would you define these traits in Prospero's personality?

E   Lines 194–265

15 What qualities, good or bad, does Caliban exhibit in this part of the scene?

16 What has Prospero achieved by the end of Act 4?

Drama

1 Working in groups of five or six, decide how you would stage the appearances of the spirits in this scene. Imagine you are the production team. The specialisms (some of which can be combined) for which you will need personnel are:
   - lighting
   - sound
   - special effects
   - costume and props
   - set designers

   You will also need a director.
   - Decide on the overall image that you want to create and then develop it to include both the goddesses and the dogs. Find some way of linking these two appearances.
   - Consider what effect a large or a small budget would have on your ideas. How would you respond to the opportunities of the first and the constraints of the second?
   - Make a presentation of your ideas to the rest of the class. This should consist of a brief talk, illustrated with diagrams and sketches for set, costumes and lighting, and an indication of the colour schemes you favour.

2 Look again at Prospero's famous speech (lines 148–158) *'Our revels now are ended ...... Is rounded with a sleep'*.

   Copy, or photocopy the lines, so that you have enough space to mark up your copy with the decisions you make together on the best ways to present it.
   - Work in pairs to learn it.
   - Listen to your partner's version and help with constructive criticism.
   - Find the rhythm and the pace of these lines.
   - Experiment with the volume – does it get louder or quieter?
   - What is the tone? Is it reflective, tired, angry, sad, pessimistic?
   - Try them all to see which works best.

Close study

Lines 1–56

1 In his first speech (lines 1–11) how does Prospero apologise to Ferdinand?
2 What phrases in Prospero's first speech convince us of his affection for, and pride in, Miranda?
3 When Prospero tells Ferdinand not to have intercourse with Miranda before the wedding his warnings are different in kind from the threats he has issued in earlier scenes. What will happen if Ferdinand disobeys?
4 Which elements in these instructions are picked up more positively in the masque?
5 What powerful images does Ferdinand use to convince Prospero that he understands what he is promising?
6 Prospero arranges for the masque and then (in lines 51–54) again speaks sternly to Ferdinand, perhaps because he and Miranda have dared to kiss or embrace. What effect is the masque likely to have?
7 How would you sum up the purpose to which Prospero has put his magic powers in previous acts? What has he always aimed to achieve? What promises to be different in his application of magic this time, in the masque?

Lines 60–117

1 What image of the countryside does Iris bring?
2 What theme is re-established in lines 84–86?
3 How does Prospero reinforce his insistence on the couple's chastity before marriage in lines 94–101?
4 Look up the full stories of the deities (gods and goddesses) mentioned in the masque, so that you may have part of the same background knowledge as Shakespeare's audience. They are:
    Iris
    Ceres
    Ceres' daughter, Prosperina
    Juno
    Dis
    Venus
    Cupid
    Mars
You will find them, (and their alternative names) in encyclopaedias, good reference dictionaries, or in a specialist reference book, for example *The Concise Oxford Companion to Classical Literature*.

Lines 139–163

As the masque comes to an abrupt end, Prospero has forgotten, not necessarily the fact of the conspiracy, but the time.

1 What must the sight of Prospero's present anger do to Ferdinand, now that he thought he was safe?

2 How does he explain his behaviour to Ferdinand this time? Is this the whole truth?

Lines 188–265

1 Do you agree with Prospero's statement in lines 188–190?

2 As in Act 3 scene 2, two of the three involved in the plot turn on the third. What is the difference this time?

3 Which of them makes Stephano turn aside from his bloodthirsty purpose?

Key speech

Lines 146–163

1 Again Prospero's attitude to Ferdinand seems to have changed: *'You do look…Be cheerful sir.'* Does this signal a new humanity?

2 There is a suggestion that in *The Tempest* Shakespeare is retiring from his role as Court playwright. What different levels of meaning can you find in *'Our revels now are ended'*?

3 What aspect of the feelings of cast, crew and director at the end of the run of a production might lines 148–150 express?

4 How in lines 152–153 do alliteration and assonance (see GLOSSARY, pages 223 and 224) combine to produce the rolling impression of glories which will pass? Be very specific in pointing out letters and syllables, and even any pauses, which achieve this.

5 Lines 151–156 speak of an ending. At one level the buildings are 'baseless' because they are part of the elaborate spectacle of the masque. What is there about this particular range of edifices, the frequent backdrop to court masques, which is designed to flatter the royal audience? Why extend it to *'the great globe itself'* and *'all which it inherit'*? What other idea might 'the great globe' return us to?

6 What is in Prospero's mind when he mentions: *'dreams'*, *'little life'*, *'a sleep'*, *'vexed'*?

7 What is the one threat remaining to him?

8 In the context of Prospero's previous treatment of Ferdinand, do you think that what he has said is enough to secure for him the understanding he asks for in lines 159–160?

Writing

1 Investigate the part played by sleep, dreams and a trance-like state in the play so far. Why for instance does Miranda need to fall asleep at that particular point in Act 1?
Think about these:
Act 1 scene 2 lines 184–186, 305–307, 325–330, 484
Act 2 scene 1 lines 181–232, 294–306
Act 3 scene 2 lines 88–89, 136–144
Act 3 scene 3 lines 5–17
Act 4 scene 1 lines 156–158

2 The masque (see page 215) is here an entertainment to celebrate the betrothal of Miranda and Ferdinand. Consider the following questions.
   - What parallel is Prospero seeking to draw here, when a masque at the Court of King James would aim to glorify the monarch?
   - What does a royal engagement signify in terms of continuity for the royal line?
   - What does the future of the young couple mean for Prospero's future?
   - How is what is promised here different from life on the island?
   - How is the language of the masque different from that of the rest of the play? How important is the fact that the verse rhymes so consistently?
   - What is significant about the fact that in the masque there is no winter, and that autumn, as shown in the reapers' dance is a time of plenty, of harvest?
   - In Milan, and on the island, Prospero has had to deal with threats to his life. Is there any reflection of these realities in the masque?
   Now write about the significance of the masque in *The Tempest* with reference to some or all of these elements:
   – the countryside it evokes
   – the fact that classical goddesses give their blessing
   – the story about Cupid
   – the verse
   – the sentiments expressed
   – the dance.

Prospero's schemes are nearing completion. Ariel reports that the King and his followers are still under a spell near Prospero's cell. Alonso, Antonio and Sebastian remain in a strange mood and Gonzalo weeps. Even Ariel, a spirit, not a human, is quite affected by it.

1 **project**: scheme, undertaking, design
gather to a head: the later stages in the development of a boil, sometimes indeed called 'a gathering'. 'Project' is also used in alchemy where a substance is thrown into or on to something to precipitate a change. Perhaps it is not too fanciful to suggest that as in alchemy Prospero is hoping to transform base matter into something more like gold

2 **crack not**: do not fail

2–3 **time Goes...his carriage**: time carries his burden with a more upright stance, now that his load is lightened (as Prospero's project nears its end)

3 **How's the day?**: what's the time

8 **gave in charge**: instructed

10 **line-grove**: group of lime trees
weather-fends: protects from rough weather

11 **till your release**: until released by you

12 **abide all three distracted**: remain mad all three

14 **Brimful**: something that is 'brimful' risks running over, as do Gonzalo's tears

17 **From eaves of reeds**: a roof thatched with reed not straw, takes on a silvery grey colour as it ages like Gonzalo's beard. Rain falls from the thatch all around the house, as it has no form of guttering

18–19 **your affections...tender**: your feelings would soften towards them

> • *How does Ariel, one of Prospero's creatures, show his compassion and affect Prospero's moral sense? Does this change in Prospero's attitude strengthen the theory that Ariel might represent part of Prospero's own nature?*

Act five

Scene 1

Before PROSPERO's *cell*

Enter PROSPERO *in his magic robes, and* ARIEL

PROSPERO   Now does my project gather to a head:
My charms crack not; my spirits obey; and time
Goes upright with his carriage. How's the day?

ARIEL   On the sixth hour; at which time, my lord,
You said our work should cease.

PROSPERO   I did say so,   5
When first I raised the tempest. Say, my spirit,
How fares the King and 's followers?

ARIEL   Confined
together
In the same fashion as you gave in charge,
Just as you left them; all prisoners, sir,
In the line-grove which weather-fends your cell; 10
They cannot budge till your release. The King,
His brother, and yours, abide all three distracted,
And the remainder mourning over them,
Brimful of sorrow and dismay; but chiefly
Him that you termed, sir, 'The good old lord,
   Gonzalo'; 15
His tears run down his beard, like winter's drops
From eaves of reeds. Your charm so strongly works
   'em
That if you now beheld them, your affections
Would become tender.

PROSPERO   Dost thou think so, spirit?

ARIEL   Mine would, sir, were I human.

Prospero, impressed by Ariel's feeling for the King and the two brothers, and by what he sees as their penitent mood, will release and forgive them. He sends Ariel to bring them to him and recalls all his powers and what he has achieved with them.

21–24 Hast thou...thou art?: if you, created out of air, have a small sense, just a slight feeling, for their sufferings, how much more sympathetically should I not be moved, someone like them who senses everything as sharply as they do and feels as deeply

24 kindlier: more sympathetically, and as part of 'humankind'

25 their high wrongs: the grave injustices they have done me
th' quick: sensitive part of the flesh in any part of the body

27 take part: side with

27–28 The rarer...vengeance: the more difficult, and therefore less freqent reaction, is to exercise moral excellence rather than vengeance, which though tempting, would just repay wrong with wrong

28–30 They...frown further: if they regret what they have done, my whole intention is that rage against them shall not continue

35 ebbing Neptune: receding tide

36 demi-puppets: doll-sized elves, also controlled like puppets, by Prospero

37 green sour ringlets: the darker ring in grass, caused by fungus growth, but believed to be where fairies dance in a round

39 midnight mushrooms: mushrooms which grow so quickly that they seem to appear overnight

40 curfew: the evening bell rung at nine o'clock

41 Weak masters though ye be: spirits low down in the hierarchy, dependent on Prospero's instructions

43–44 'twixt...roaring war: I have made tumultuous storms rage between sea and sky

45 rifted: split
Jove's stout oak: the oak tree was sacred to Jove

46 With his own bolt: it was Jove who was also the god of thunder and lightning

47 spurs: roots

48–50 Graves...art: this is not an area of magic we have seen on the island. Prospero may be talking about earlier experiments

50 rough magic: magic which is visible, almost in the form of 'magic tricks'

51 abjure: renounce
required: requested

53 mine end: my purpose

• *What is Prospero giving up?*

PROSPERO   And mine shall. 20
           Hast thou, which art but air, a touch, a feeling
           Of their afflictions, and shall not myself,
           One of their kind, that relish all as sharply,
           Passion as they, be kindlier moved than thou art?
           Though with their high wrongs I am struck to th'
                 quick,   25
           Yet with my nobler reason, 'gainst my fury
           Do I take part. The rarer action is
           In virtue than in vengeance. They being penitent,
           The sole drift of my purpose doth extend
           Not a frown further. Go release them Ariel.   30
           My charms I'll break, their senses I'll restore,
           And they shall be themselves.

ARIEL   I'll fetch them,
                 sir.   [*Exit*

PROSPERO   Ye elves of hills, brooks, standing lakes, and groves,
           And ye that on the sands with printless foot
           Do chase the ebbing Neptune, and do fly him   35
           When he comes back; you demi-puppets that
           By moonshine do the green sour ringlets make,
           Whereof the ewe not bites; and you whose pastime
           Is to make midnight mushrooms, that rejoice
           To hear the solemn curfew; by whose aid –   40
           Weak masters though ye be – I have bedimmed
           The noontide sun, called forth the mutinous winds,
           And 'twixt the green sea and the azured vault
           Set roaring war. To the dread rattling thunder
           Have I given fire, and rifted Jove's stout oak   45
           With his own bolt. The strong-based promontory
           Have I made shake, and by the spurs plucked up
           The pine and cedar. Graves at my command
           Have waked their sleepers, oped, and let 'em forth
           By my so potent art. But this rough magic   50
           I here abjure; and when I have required
           Some heavenly music – which even now I do –
           To work mine end upon their senses that

Prospero says he will break his magician's staff and bury it and throw his book into the sea. When the royal party has entered the magic circle he has drawn, he starts to restore their addled senses. Then he praises Gonzalo and accuses the others of the misdeeds they have committed or planned to commit.

54 This airy charm: both 'this charm which is in the air' and 'this charm accompanied by music'

55 fathoms: a fathom was a measure of a man's outstretched arms, roughly six feet (1.82 m)

58–59 A solemn air...cure thy brains: may solemn music, the best means of soothing a troubled imagination, make your brains normal again

59 boiled: which are still seething in your skull

63 sociable...of thine: sympathetic to what I see in yours

64 Fall fellowly drops: let fall companionable tears
    apace: speedily

67–68 the ignorant fumes...reason: the mists of ignorance which screen from them their ability to reason clearly

69 sir: gentleman

70–71 pay thy graces...word and deed: acknowledge and repay in a practical way your good deeds

74 pinched: tormented, with a suggestion of both the mental and physical pain involved in punishment. Caliban, of course, knows about actual pinches

76 Expelled remorse and nature: drove out remorse and the natural feelings of a brother

77 inward pinches: agonies of conscience

80 Begins to swell: like the incoming tide, their true understanding starts to rise

> • *The revelation about the plot to kill Alonso is news to all on stage except the plotters. Is the rest of the party in a fit state to take it in? In addition, line 73 contains the first accusation that Sebastian was involved in ousting Prospero from Milan.*

This airy charm is for, I'll break my staff,
Bury it certain fathoms in the earth,   55
And deeper than did ever plummet sound
I'll drown my book.   [*Solemn music*

Enter ARIEL *before: then* ALONSO, *with a frantic*
gesture, attended by GONZALO; SEBASTIAN *and*
ANTONIO *in like manner, attended by* ADRIAN *and*
FRANCISCO: *they all enter the circle which* PROSPERO
had made, and there stand charmed; which
PROSPERO *observing, speaks*

A solemn air, and the best comforter
To an unsettled fancy, cure thy brains,
Now useless, boiled within thy skull. There
    stand,   60
For you are spell-stopped.
Holy Gonzalo, honourable man,
Mine eyes, even sociable to the show of thine,
Fall fellowly drops. The charm dissolves apace,
And as the morning steals upon the night,   65
Melting the darkness, so their rising senses
Begin to chase the ignorant fumes that mantle
Their clearer reason. O good Gonzalo,
My true preserver, and a loyal sir
To him thou follow'st, I will pay thy graces   70
Home both in word and deed. Most cruelly
Didst thou, Alonso, use me and my daughter;
Thy brother was a furtherer in the act.
Thou art pinched for 't now Sebastian. Flesh and
    blood,
You, brother mine, that entertained ambition,   75
Expelled remorse and nature; who, with Sebastian –
Whose inward pinches therefore are most strong –
Would here have killed your King; I do forgive
    thee,
Unnatural though thou art. Their understanding
Begins to swell, and the approaching tide   80

Because Alonso and even his own brother do not recognise him, Prospero takes off his magic robes and wears the gentleman's accessories he would have worn in Milan. Again promising Ariel freedom, he tells him to fetch the master of the boat and the boatswain. Prospero reveals himself as the 'wronged Duke of Milan'.

81 **Will shortly…shore**: this rising tide of understanding will soon fill the shore of their reason, which at present is smelly and muddy

82–83 **Not one…know me**: there is not one of them who can focus on me yet, or who would recognise me if he could. They are still dazed by magic

85 **discase me**: take off my magic robes

86 **As I was…Milan**: as I looked once, as Duke of Milan

90 **couch**: lie

91–92 **on the bat's…After summer**: the suggestion is that Ariel will follow summer where it is to be found. Bats are not known to migrate

96 **So, so, so**: possibly straightening his ducal clothes

101 **presently**: straightaway

103 **Or ere**: before

105 **Some heavenly power guide**: may some heavenly etc

108 **For more assurance**: to give you added conviction

112 **some enchanted…abuse me**: some magic apparition to deceive me

Will shortly fill the reasonable shore
That now lies foul and muddy. Not one of them
That yet looks on me, or would know me. Ariel,
Fetch me the hat and rapier in my cell.
I will discase me, and myself present   85
As I was sometime Milan. Quickly spirit,
Thou shalt ere long be free.

ARIEL *sings, and helps to attire him*

    Where the bee sucks, there suck I.
    In a cowslip's bell I lie;
    There I couch when owls do cry.   90
    On the bat's back I do fly
    After summer merrily.
   Merrily, merrily shall I live now
   Under the blossom that hangs on the bough.

PROSPERO   Why, that's my dainty Ariel. I shall miss thee,   95
But yet thou shalt have freedom. So, so, so.
To the King's ship, invisible as thou art.
There shalt thou find the mariners asleep
Under the hatches. The master and the boatswain
Being awake, enforce them to this place,   100
And presently, I prithee.

ARIEL   I drink the air before me, and return
Or ere your pulse twice beat.   [*Exit*

GONZALO   All torment, trouble, wonder and amazement
Inhabits here. Some heavenly power guide us   105
Out of this fearful country.

PROSPERO   Behold, sir King,
The wronged Duke of Milan, Prospero.
For more assurance that a living prince
Does now speak to thee, I embrace thy body;
And to thee and thy company I bid   110
A hearty welcome.

ALONSO   Whether thou be'st he or no,
Or some enchanted trifle to abuse me,

Alonso, who feels his madness leaving him, asks Prospero's pardon. Prospero embraces Gonzalo. In an aside he reminds Antonio and Sebastian that he knows about their proposed treachery and could tell Alonso about it. He specifically forgives Antonio but demands the restitution of his dukedom. Alonso wants to hear the whole story and then remembers the loss of his son.

113 **late**: recently

115 **Th' affliction of my mind amends**: the confusion my mind was in, is improving

116 **crave**: demand

118 **Thy dukedom I resign**: Alonso, by joining in Antonio's scheming, had acquired the right to tribute from Milan

120 **First, noble friend**: Prospero turns first to Gonzalo

123–124 do yet taste...th' isle: still are under the influence of some illusions of the island. 'Subtilties' were also elaborately decorated sugar confectionery at banquets of the time. 'Taste' would work for both meanings

126 **brace**: pair

127–128 could pluck...traitors: I could bring the King's displeasure on you and prove that you are traitors

129 **The devil...him**: the only way that Sebastian can account for Prospero's knowledge
No: Prospero, as magician, may have heard this aside and is denying it, as briefly as it deserves; or he is confirming 'no tales'

132 **rankest**: most foul
require: ask, but with the force of 'demand'

133 **perforce**: of necessity – he will have to give it back when the rightful duke appears

139 **woe**: sorry, grieved

> • *Notice Prospero's first direct greeting to Gonzalo – he speaks to him rather than acknowledging Alonso's request for forgiveness.*

As late I have been, I not know. Thy pulse
Beats, as of flesh and blood. And, since I saw thee,
Th' affliction of my mind amends, with which,   115
I fear a madness held me. This must crave –
An if this be at all – a most strange story.
Thy dukedom I resign, and do entreat
Thou pardon me my wrongs. But how should
        Prospero
Be living and be here?

PROSPERO   First, noble friend,   120
Let me embrace thine age, whose honour cannot
Be measured or confined.

GONZALO   Whether this be
Or be not, I'll not swear.

PROSPERO   You do yet taste
Some subtilties o' th' isle, that will not let you
Believe things certain. Welcome, my friends all.   125
[*Aside to* SEBASTIAN *and* ANTONIO] But you, my
        brace of lords, were I so minded,
I here could pluck his highness' frown upon you
And justify you traitors. At this time
I will tell no tales.

SEBASTIAN   [*Aside*]   The devil speaks in him.

PROSPERO   No.
For you, most wicked sir, whom to call brother   130
Would even infect my mouth, I do forgive
Thy rankest fault – all of them; and require
My dukedom of thee, which perforce I know,
Thou must restore.

ALONSO   If thou be'st Prospero,
Give us particulars of thy preservation;   135
How thou hast met us here, who three hours since
Were wrecked upon this shore; where I have lost –
How sharp the point of this remembrance is –
My dear son Ferdinand.

PROSPERO   I am woe for 't, sir.

While Alonso grieves over the loss of Ferdinand, Prospero claims he has suffered a similar loss – that of his daughter. The rest of the party can hardly believe their eyes and ears. Prospero assures them that he was the Duke of Milan, is the lord of the island, and will reveal the story to them in due course.

142 **of whose soft grace**: thanks to her mercy (that of patience)
143 **like**: similar
   sovereign: supreme
145 **as late**: and as recent
145–147 **supportable...comfort you**: to make my precious loss bearable I have only feebler means for comfort than you have. Alonso still has his daughter and Prospero knows that Ferdinand and Miranda will be in Naples while he is alone in Milan
149 **that they were**: if only they were
151 **mudded in that oozy bed**: buried in that muddy sea-bed
154 **At this encounter...admire**: at this meeting are so amazed
155 **That they devour their reason**: that they seem to have swallowed their powers of reasoning
155–156 **and scarce think...of truth**: they can hardly believe their eyes
156–157 **their words...breath**: they cannot speak (they are gaping in amazement and can only expel their breath, no words come out)
157 **howsoe'er**: to whatever degree
158 **justled**: shaken
160 **thrust forth of**: cast out from
167 **abroad**: elsewhere on the island
168 **My dukedom...again**: since you have restored my dukedom to me

ALONSO   Irreparable is the loss, and patience   140
            Says it is past her cure.

PROSPERO   I rather think
            You have not sought her help, of whose soft grace
            For the like loss I have her sovereign aid,
            And rest myself content.

ALONSO   You the like loss?

PROSPERO   As great to me as late; and, supportable   145
            To make the dear loss, have I means much weaker
            Than you may call to comfort you, for I
            Have lost my daughter.

ALONSO   A daughter?
            O heavens, that they were living both in Naples,
            The king and queen there. That they were, I
                wish   150
            Myself were mudded in that oozy bed
            Where my son lies. When did you lose your
                daughter?

PROSPERO   In this last tempest. I perceive these lords
            At this encounter do so much admire,
            That they devour their reason, and scarce think 155
            Their eyes do offices of truth, their words
            Are natural breath. But howsoe'er you have
            Been justled from your senses, know for certain
            That I am Prospero, and that very duke
            Which was thrust forth of Milan, who most
                strangely   160
            Upon this shore, where you were wrecked, was
                landed,
            To be the lord on 't. No more yet of this;
            For 'tis a chronicle of day by day,
            Not a relation for a breakfast, nor
            Befitting this first meeting. Welcome, sir,   165
            This cell's my court. Here have I few attendants,
            And subjects none abroad. Pray you look in.
            My dukedom since you have given me again,

Prospero reveals Ferdinand and Miranda who are playing chess.
Alonso hardly dares believe his eyes. Ferdinand kneels to him for
his blessing and introduces Miranda.

169 **requite you with**: give you in return
170 **bring forth a wonder**: again a punning reference to Miranda's
   name and the possibility that Prospero has now produced such a
   scene without the aid of magic
   [***discovers***: reveals. Chess was then considered an aristocratic game
   – because the pieces are kings, queens, knights, etc. It was quite
   proper for a young man and woman to play in private, without a
   chaperone]
172 **you play me false**: Miranda jokily accuses Ferdinand of cheating.
   He denies this in the next line
174–175 **Yes, for a score...fair play**: she picks up his casual 'not for
   the world' and asserts that he would battle with her even if it were
   not the world at stake but only a few kingdoms. She wouldn't
   mind she says – the understanding being because she loves him
176 **A vision...island**: another of the illusions Alonso is becoming used
   to
177 **A most high miracle**: either a sardonic comment on the
   disappearance of his hopes for the crown of Naples, or an attempt
   to ingratiate himself with Prospero
180 **compass thee about**: surround you
184 **'Tis new to thee**: a cynical comment from Prospero who has seen
   the evil side of the world
185 **at play**: playing chess
186 **Your eld'st...three hours**: the longest you can possibly have
   known her is only three hours
187 **severed us**: parted us (in the storm)

I will requite you with as good a thing;
At least bring forth a wonder, to content ye   170
As much as me my dukedom.

Here PROSPERO *discovers* FERDINAND *and* MIRANDA
playing at chess

MIRANDA   Sweet lord, you play me false.

FERDINAND   No my dearest love,
I would not for the world.

MIRANDA   Yes, for a score of kingdoms you should wrangle,
And I would call it fair play.

ALONSO   If this prove   175
A vision of the island, one dear son
Shall I twice lose.

SEBASTIAN   A most high miracle.

FERDINAND   Though the seas threaten, they are merciful.
I have cursed them without cause.   [*Kneels*

ALONSO   Now all the
        blessings
Of a glad father compass thee about.   180
Arise, and say how thou camest here.

MIRANDA   O wonder!
How many goodly creatures are there here.
How beauteous mankind is. O brave new world
That has such people in 't!

PROSPERO   'Tis new to thee.

ALONSO   What is this maid with whom thou wast at play?   185
Your eld'st acquaintance cannot be three hours.
Is she the goddess that hath severed us,
And brought us thus together?

FERDINAND   Sir, she is mortal;
But by immortal Providence she's mine.
I chose her when I could not ask my father   190
For his advice, nor thought I had one. She
Is daughter to this famous Duke of Milan,

Ferdinand explains to Alonso that as he and Miranda are engaged, he now has a second father in Prospero. Alonso will fill the same role for Miranda. Gonzalo calls down blessings on the couple and finds that everyone has gained something. Ariel brings in the master of the ship and the boatswain.

193 **Of whom...renown**: whose reputation I have so often heard about
196 **1 am hers**: 1 am her second father too
198 **Must...forgiveness**: Alonso will have to ask Miranda's forgiveness for sending the then three-year-old to almost certain death
199–200 **Let us not...that's gone**: Prospero suggests that former sadness should no longer weigh down their memories
200 **inly**: inwardly
203 **chalked forth the way**: marked out the path
208 **With gold...pillars**: as a lasting and public commemoration
213 **When...his own**: when no one was himself
214 **still**: for ever
[*amazedly*: in a bewildered, confused state]

- *Is Gonzalo ascribing to the gods what has really been engineered by Prospero? Is there any difference?*
- *In lines 214–215 Alonso is calling down a curse, but who are the two men who certainly do not 'wish them joy'?*

Of whom so often I have heard renown,
But never saw before; of whom I have
Received a second life; and second father   195
This lady makes him to me.

ALONSO   I am hers.
But O, how oddly will it sound that I
Must ask my child forgiveness.

PROSPERO   There, sir, stop.
Let us not burden our remembrance with
A heaviness that's gone.

GONZALO   I have inly wept,   200
Or should have spoke ere this. Look down you
     gods,
And on this couple drop a blessed crown;
For it is you that have chalked forth the way
Which brought us hither.

ALONSO   I say Amen, Gonzalo.

GONZALO   Was Milan thrust from Milan, that his issue   205
Should become kings of Naples? O rejoice
Beyond a common joy, and set it down
With gold on lasting pillars. In one voyage
Did Claribel her husband find at Tunis,
And Ferdinand, her brother, found a wife,   210
Where he himself was lost, Prospero his dukedom
In a poor isle, and all of us ourselves
When no man was his own.

ALONSO   [*To* FERDINAND *and* MIRANDA] Give me your hands.
Let grief and sorrow still embrace his heart.
That doth not wish you joy.

GONZALO   Be it so, Amen.   215

Enter ARIEL, *with the* MASTER *and* BOATSWAIN
amazedly following

O look sir, look, sir. Here is more of us.
I prophesied, if a gallows were on land,

The master and the boatswain, reunited with the king and company, bring the news that their ship, apparently split in the storm, is now as good as new. Ariel tells Prospero that he has achieved all this and the two sailors describe their release.

218 blasphemy: Prospero uses this noun as though it is the boatswain's name
219 That...o'erboard: you who swear until all grace leaves the ship
223 but three glasses since: just three hours ago (timed by using an hour glass)
we gave out split: we declared had been split
224 tight and yare and bravely rigged: watertight, trim and her rigging sound
226 tricksy: full of tricks, cunning, ingenious
227–228 strengthen...stranger: they are becoming more and more strange
231 clapped: shut
232 but even now: just a few moments ago
234 moe: more
236 Where we...beheld: where we, in clothes that seemed fresh, gazed afresh or took a fresh look at... This may be a transferred epithet – 'we freshly beheld' for 'we beheld our fresh ship'. Compare it with 'The travellers relaxed in the grateful warmth of the fire'. The warmth wasn't grateful, the travellers were
238 Capering to eye her: dancing with delight at the sight of her
On a trice: in an instant
240 moping: in a dazed state, in a state of bewilderment
241 my diligence: my diligent Ariel. Again, as in line 218 the adjective is turned into the descriptive, but abstract, noun. Compare also Prospero's calling Caliban 'malice' in Act 1 scene 2, because he finds him malicious

> • *The boatswain's evidence 'three glasses since' confirms that the action of the play has taken place in 'real time'. See page 209 for a note on the Unities (of time, place and action).*

This fellow could not drown. Now blasphemy,
That swear'st grace o'erboard, not an oath on
 shore?
Hast thou no mouth by land? What is the
 news?   220

BOATSWAIN   The best news is, that we have safely found
Our King and company; the next, our ship,
Which but three glasses since, we gave out split,
Is tight and yare and bravely rigged, as when
We first put out to sea.

ARIEL   [*Aside to* PROSPERO]   Sir, all this service   225
Have I done since I went.

PROSPERO   [*Aside to* ARIEL]   My tricksy spirit.

ALONSO   These are not natural events, they strengthen
From stranger to stranger. Say, how came you
 hither?

BOATSWAIN   If I did think, sir, I were well awake,
I 'ld strive to tell you. We were dead of sleep,   230
And – how we know not – all clapped under
 hatches,
Where, but even now with strange and several
 noises
Of roaring, shrieking, howling, jingling chains,
And moe diversity of sounds, all horrible,
We were awaked; straightway, at liberty;   235
Where we, in all our trim, freshly beheld
Our royal, good, and gallant ship; our master
Capering to eye her. On a trice, so please you,
Even in a dream, were we divided from them,
And were brought moping hither.

ARIEL   [*Aside to* PROSPERO]   Was 't well
 done?   240

PROSPERO   [*Aside to* ARIEL] Bravely, my diligence. Thou shalt
 be free.

ALONSO   This is as strange a maze as e'er men trod,

Alonso is still amazed and puzzled at all these events. Prospero promises that everything will be explained and instructs Ariel to release Caliban, Stephano and Trinculo. Caliban is impressed by the company and afraid of Prospero's punishment.

243–244 more than…conduct of: more than any natural occurrences could contrive

245 rectify our knowledge: correct and re-order our understanding
my liege: it is not clear why Prospero should address Alonso as 'my liege' since it means 'sovereign lord', to whom the speaker owes allegiance. It is either a courtesy title or owing to the fact that, until matters are regulated, Milan is still held subject to Naples

246 infest your mind: harass, trouble your mind
beating on: hammering away at

247 at picked leisure: at a leisure moment of our choice

248 Which shall…you: which shall be soon, I will, in private, give you a plausible explanation of all these events

256 Every man…the rest: we're all in this together. The assumption is that Stephano is saying the opposite of what he really feels which is 'every man for himself', but he is very drunk

257 for all is but fortune: it's all in the luck of the draw
Coragio: the Italian for 'Courage!'

258 bully: a term of affection, used almost as a title. (Compare the greeting Bottom the weaver receives from his fellows 'bully Bottom' in *A Midsummer Night's Dream*)

259 If these be…head: if I can trust what my eyes are reporting back to me

261 Setebos: Caliban's god
brave: fine, splendid

266 a plain fish: plainly, clearly, a fish

267 badges: servants of noble families would wear the family's crest or other heraldic device embroidered on their livery (uniform). While Trinculo and Stephano may still be wearing some of their usual clothes, they may have added items of clothing taken from the line – a livery proclaiming theft

268 true: honest, good

> • *Where else have we seen this desire to exploit what is found in a foreign country?*

And there is in this business more than nature
Was ever conduct of. Some oracle
Must rectify our knowledge.

PROSPERO   Sir, my liege,   245
Do not infest your mind with beating on
The strangeness of this business; at picked leisure,
Which shall be shortly, single I'll resolve you,
Which to you shall seem probable, of every
These happened accidents; till when, be
        cheerful,   250
And think of each thing well. [*Aside to* ARIEL]
        Come hither spirit:
Set Caliban and his companions free;
Untie the spell. [*Exit* ARIEL] How fares my gracious
        sir?
There are yet missing of your company
Some few odd lads that you remember not.   255

Enter ARIEL, *driving in* CALIBAN, STEPHANO, *and*
TRINCULO, *in their stolen apparel*

STEPHANO   Every man shift for all the rest, and let no man take
care for himself; for all is but fortune. Coragio
bully-monster, coragio!

TRINCULO   If these be true spies which I wear in my head,
here's a goodly sight.   260

CALIBAN   O Setebos, these be brave spirits indeed.
How fine my master is. I am afraid
He will chastise me.

SEBASTIAN   Ha, ha!
What things are these, my lord Antonio?
Will money buy 'em?

ANTONIO   Very like. One of them   265
Is a plain fish, and no doubt marketable.

PROSPERO   Mark but the badges of these men, my lords,
Then say if they be true. This mis-shapen knave,
His mother was a witch, and one so strong

Prospero explains who Caliban is and Alonso and Sebastian recognise the other two. Prospero dismisses all three, telling Caliban to prepare his cell for the visitors.

270 control the moon...ebbs: Sycorax even had power over the moon and, like it, could control the ebb and flow of tides

271 And deal...power: make commands as she (the moon) could, quite outside her normal areas of power; i.e. Sycorax could control the moon to such an extent that, having at her command the moon's authority, she could perform what was normally beyond the scope of the moon's powers ('without' meaning 'outside' or 'beyond'. Modern Scottish English 'outwith' has the same sense)

275 know and own: recognise and claim as yours
thing of darkness: either Caliban's dark skin colour, or that he is in Prospero's eyes evil as he tried to rape Miranda, or that he is unenlightened because Prospero's attempts at education seem to have failed – or something of all three

275–276 I Acknowledge mine: I must take responsibility for

279 reeling ripe: so drunk he cannot walk straight but reels about

280 gilded: (here) flushed. (In *Macbeth* 'gild' is used when Lady Macbeth smears the King's sentries with blood to suggest that they have killed him)

281 pickle: a mess, or vegetables or fish preserved in vinegar; being 'pickled' – preserved in alcohol, still means drunk

284 fear fly-blowing: blow-flies are unlikely to lay their eggs on anything pickled

286 a cramp: just one pain all over

287 sirrah: form of address used to inferiors, particularly when they are considered to have misbehaved

290–291 He is...his shape: just as we find his shape ugly and defective, so is his behaviour

293 trim it handsomely: prepare it well and make it neat

295 seek for grace: try to obtain forgiveness

298 bestow your luggage: put back that stuff you've been carrying around

> • *In acknowledging 'this thing of darkness' as his, is Prospero admitting responsibility for what Caliban has become, and therefore for the darker side of his own nature?*

	That could control the moon, make flows and	
	ebbs,	270
	And deal in her command without her power.	
	These three have robbed me, and this demi-devil –	
	For he's a bastard one – had plotted with them	
	To take my life. Two of these fellows you	
	Must know and own; this thing of darkness I	275
	Acknowledge mine.	

CALIBAN   I shall be pinched to death.

ALONSO   Is not this Stephano, my drunken butler?

SEBASTIAN   He is drunk now. Where had he wine?

ALONSO   And Trinculo is reeling ripe. Where should they
Find this grand liquor that hath gilded 'em?   280
How cam'st thou in this pickle?

TRINCULO   I have been in such a pickle since I saw you last
that, I fear me, will never out of my bones. I shall
not fear fly-blowing.

SEBASTIAN   Why how now Stephano.   285

STEPHANO   O touch me not, I am not Stephano, but a cramp.

PROSPERO   You'd be king o' th' isle, sirrah?

STEPHANO   I should have been a sore one then.

ALONSO   This is a strange thing as e'er I look'd on.
                                        [*Pointing to* CALIBAN

PROSPERO   He is as disproportioned in his manners   290
As in his shape. Go sirrah, to my cell,
Take with you your companions. As you look
To have my pardon, trim it handsomely.

CALIBAN   Ay, that I will. And I'll be wise hereafter,
And seek for grace. What a thrice-double ass   295
Was I to take this drunkard for a god,
And worship this dull fool.

PROSPERO   Go to, away.

ALONSO   Hence, and bestow your luggage where you found
it.

Prospero invites the King and his company to spend the night in his cell. He promises to tell the story of his life on the island and then they will all set sail for Italy on the following morning, catching up the rest of the King's fleet. When they have all left the stage, Prospero returns to deliver an epilogue to the audience, asking, now that he has given up magic, that they shall release him from the island.

300 **your train**: the rest of your company
302 **waste**: spend
305 **accidents**: events, happenings
308–309 **nuptial...solemnized**: marriage service
311 **Every third...my grave**: Prospero has mastered strange areas of magic, which would scandalise the Catholic church. Having renounced sorcery he must begin to prepare himself to make what the Holy Church would call 'a good death' and will devote a third of his contemplation to this end
314 **auspicious gales**: favourable winds
315 **sail so expeditious**: such speedy sailing
317–318 **Then to...Be free**: take for yourself the freedom of the elements, to which you belong

Prospero addresses the audience: his magic is at an end and he will have to remain on the island unless the audience release him through the power of their applause.

2 **mine own**: the same powers that any clever and resourceful man might claim to have
4 **confined**: if the audience does not give him 'a fair wind' he will be confined as he has confined Ariel, Caliban and the King's party
7 **And pardoned the deceiver**: he sees the pardon he has extended to Antonio as speaking well for him with the audience and with God

SEBASTIAN	Or stole it rather. [*Exeunt* CALIBAN, STEPHANO,
	and TRINCULO
PROSPERO	Sir, I invite your Highness, and your train 300
	To my poor cell, where you shall take your rest
	For this one night, which, part of it, I'll waste
	With such discourse as, I not doubt, shall make it
	Go quick away; the story of my life,
	And the particular accidents gone by 305
	Since I came to this isle. And in the morn
	I'll bring you to your ship, and so to Naples,
	Where I have hope to see the nuptial
	Of these our dear-beloved solemnized;
	And thence retire me to my Milan, where 310
	Every third thought shall be my grave.
ALONSO	I long
	To hear the story of your life, which must
	Take the ear strangely.
PROSPERO	I'll deliver all,
	And promise you calm seas, auspicious gales,
	And sail so expeditious that shall catch 315
	Your royal fleet far off. [*Aside to* ARIEL] My Ariel,
	chick,
	That is thy charge. Then to the elements
	Be free, and fare thou well. Please you draw near.
	[*Exeunt*

EPILOGUE
Spoken by PROSPERO

Now my charms are all o'erthrown,
And what strength I have's mine own,
Which is most faint. Now, 'tis true
I must be here confined by you,
Or sent to Naples. Let me not,   5
Since I have my dukedom got,
And pardoned the deceiver, dwell
In this bare island by your spell;

Prospero continues his request to the audience for applause, saying he set out to please them. He no longer has spirits to do his bidding so he asks for the prayers and the indulgence of the audience.

9 **bands**: bonds
10 **With the help...hands**: with your applause and with the noise – just as he had asked for silence so that earlier magic could go ahead, noise may now break the spell
11 **Gentle breath**: kind words
13 **want**: lack, have no
15 **my ending is despair**: a serious sin entailing the loss of faith in redemption
16 **relieved by prayer**: rescued by your prayers
17–18 **pierces so...Mercy itself**: has such penetration that it is able to plead powerfully with God's mercy
18 **frees all faults**: because Christ's death on the cross was to sacrifice himself so that all human sin was capable of being forgiven. Therefore an appeal to God's mercy will bring Prospero forgiveness
20 **indulgence**: kindness, generosity and the remission of punishment for sin

But release me from my bands
With the help of your good hands.   10
Gentle breath of yours my sails
Must fill, or else my project fails,
Which was to please. Now I want
Spirits to enforce, art to enchant,
And my ending is despair,   15
Unless I be relieved by prayer,
Which pierces so, that it assaults
Mercy itself, and frees all faults.
As you from crimes would pardoned be,
Let your indulgence set me free.   20

                        [*Exit*

CTIVITIES

Keeping track

1 What has happened to Alonso and the others?
2 How have Alonso, Sebastian and Antonio been affected?
3 Why is Gonzalo weeping?
4 What remark does Ariel make about them?
5 What effect does his remark have on Prospero?
6 On what does Prospero's forgiveness of his enemies seem to depend?
7 Left alone, Prospero looks back over the magic he has created. What does he do then?
8 Prospero calls Gonzalo *'My true preserver'* (line 69). What else does he point out, and why?
9 What two indications of his rank does Prospero need in order to show the others who he really is?
10 Where have the sailors been all afternoon?
11 What potential blackmail threat does Prospero hold over Sebastian and Antonio?
12 Does Antonio declare his repentance?
13 What does Alonso anticipate in lines 149–150?
14 Why must Alonso ask Miranda's forgiveness?
15 What is strange about the ship we believed to be split?
16 How does the royal party react to the sight of Caliban?
17 What are Prospero's future plans?
18 Why, in the epilogue, does Prospero claim to need the help of the audience?

Discussion

A Lines 1–32
1 We have reached a point in the play where Prospero's enemies are entirely at his mercy. They have been physically at his mercy before.
  • What is different this time?
  • Why does Prospero need to reassure himself that his magic is still in good working order?
2 In the Bible we are told that penitence will bring God's forgiveness.
  • What echo of this do we find in this speech?
  • What does this suggest about Prospero?
  • Has this aspect of Prospero been in evidence elsewhere in the play?
  • Is Antonio penitent? Is he forgiven?

3 We learnt in Act 1 about the wrongs done to Prospero.
  • Has he taken any vengeance on the wrongdoers?
  • Is forgiveness a kind of vengeance?
4 The action of the play from the wreck to the present moment has taken about three hours. This contrasts with the twelve years for which we needed the lengthy exposition in Act 1 scene 2.
  • How necessary is the relative speed of the action for our enjoyment of the drama?
  • Bearing this speed in mind, what function do the interludes of sleep, the banquet produced by the 'shapes', Ariel's harpy act and the masque seem to have in terms of the dramatic structure?

B Lines 33–79
5 Why does Prospero find it necessary to run through a list of what he has been able to do?
6 What problems do you think he is likely to face if he gives up magic for good?

C Lines 123–134
7 Prospero has a blackmailing hold over Sebastian and Antonio.
  • How might this come in useful on their return to Italy? Under what circumstances might Prospero use it?
  • Do you think he is more likely to use it if he has given up magic?
  • If Prospero were ever to reveal the traitorous intentions of his brother and of Alonso's, what would their punishment probably be?

D Lines 215–241
8 How well have the boatswain and the master survived their experiences? What was it that most amazed them?

E Lines 261–297
9 What are the differences in the treatment Prospero offers Antonio and Caliban for their crimes? Can you decide how and why these differences are significant?
10 Are there any differences in Antonio's and Caliban's responses to Prospero?
11 What further light do your reactions to 9 and 10 throw on the debate about whether nature or nurture is the more important in forming character and personality?
12 What will happen to Caliban when Prospero and the others set sail for Naples?

Drama

1   Imagine that when Antonio returns to Milan and is faced with giving up his power he accuses Prospero of 'crimes against humanity' and 'the wicked and irresponsible use of magic' on the island.

As a whole group activity you are asked to set up a preliminary hearing to decide whether the matter should go to trial. You will need:

- Prospero
- a prosecutor
- a defender for Prospero
- witnesses, to fact and to character.

Start with a prosecution case with witnesses against Prospero.

These witnesses should then be cross-examined in an attempt to find the gaps in their claims or a more favourable side to Prospero's treatment of them.

The defence case should then be put in a similar way.

The most important witness for Prospero will probably be Miranda. It will be as important to observe the way she behaves (since Prospero has been the sole person responsible for her upbringing) as to listen to the content of what she says.

The whole group, having watched and listened carefully should then come out of role and vote on the outcome.

Close study

Lines 7–32

The question which immediately precedes Ariel's answer is similar to many of Prospero's checks with Ariel throughout the play on the progress of the plans.

1   What is different about Ariel's answer this time? Does he just give an account of what he has done? Pick out the words and phrases of Ariel's which convey the emotions he has observed.

2   If it lasted, would madness be a fair punishment for the three royal criminals? Is this temporary madness perhaps necessary to show Prospero that it is a nobler course to allow his 'reason' to rule over his fury?

3   Why are the others *'mourning over them'*? Were they popular?

4   Gonzalo has been the positive spokesman in the royal party. Why is he weeping now? What has changed? Why *'winter's drops'*? What would probably make this image (lines 16–17) more effective for Shakespeare's audience than for a present-day one?

5 Until now Ariel has shown a gleeful mischief in the roles he has been asked to play. What attitude does he show now towards his victims and, by implication – *'Your charm so strongly works 'em'* – towards Prospero?

6 What is remarkable about Ariel's reply, *'Mine would, sir, were I human'*?

7 In lines 17–27 we can empathise with Ariel over Prospero's victims, and with Prospero over himself as victim. What two feelings does Prospero claim as a result of the wrongs done to him? Have we seen evidence of these in the action of the play?

8 What is the importance of reason (line 26)? What is it opposed to in Prospero's mind? What does the exercise of his reason help him to do?

Lines 68–79

1 Why does Prospero make a point of bracketing these two facts about Gonzalo *'My true preserver, and a loyal sir To him thou follow'st'*?

2 What is meant by *'nature'* in line 76, and what force does *'Unnatural'* have in line 79?

Lines 114–139

1 Once Alonso feels he has come to his senses, what is his first impulse? How does Prospero react to what Alonso says? Why might this be?

2 Prospero's demand for the restoration of his dukedom is made directly to Antonio. How does his brother respond? What effect might you reasonably expect this to have on the final outcome?

Lines 200–240

1 What aspects of his nature, his beliefs and his understanding come out in this speech of Gonzalo's (lines 200–213)?

2 Alonso, whose return to something approaching normality is very recent, is suddenly faced with yet more marvels. How does he react to the news of his son's engagement to the young woman he so cruelly exiled as a child?

Lines 261–266

1 Caliban is thoroughly disillusioned with his new god and new master. How do we know?

2 What is noticeable about Sebastian and Antonio as they briefly rejoin the conversation at last? Are they part of the general rejoicing? What is their private exchange about?

Key speech

(A) Lines 33–57

Lines 33–40 show Prospero conjuring up these spirits to bear witness to what he is saying.

1 What does Prospero feel about this list?
- nostalgia
- regret
- impatience
- shame
- achievement
- failure
- any other sensation?

2 Those who suggest that this is also Shakespeare taking leave of his life in the theatre will look at this list differently. What would they see?

3 Has Prospero's mastery of magic achieved everything he hoped for?

4 In lines 50–57 Prospero gives up *'this rough magic'* and promises to destroy his book and his staff. What does this suggest about his future intentions? Is he different in any way from the man who landed on the island twelve years ago? What have we seen his magic used for in the course of the play?

(B) The epilogue

1 In line 317 Ariel is charged with sending the royal ship home. In what way does this seem to have changed by line 5 of the epilogue?

2 Something else seems to have changed hands as well (line 8). What?

3 What does *'confined'* (line 4) immediately remind us of?
The same idea occurs in lines 7 and in lines 19–20. How would you express it?

4 Lines 9–13 can be interpreted purely at the level of actors and director who have tried to please their audience. It is a conventional request, but what words link it specifically to this play?

5 Lines 13–20 are obviously spoken directly to the audience, as Prospero leaves the scene of his magical triumphs for ever. On an occasion when his royal patron was foremost in the audience, what else could these words signify?

Writing

1 There are many fairy-tale elements in the story of *The Tempest*; actions – even when not affected by magic – do not seem to have normal consequences; wickedness is discovered and challenged; there are strange spectacles. Using the traditional form: 'Once upon a time…lived happily ever after' write the story to be read aloud to children aged 6–8. Exchange your finished story with a partner and comment on the level of interest and appropriate use of language in each other's work.

2 Miranda and Ferdinand now have the blessing of their fathers, but what is the naively innocent Miranda likely to face once she arrives in Naples as the prospective wife of the crown prince? Write either:
   • An official welcome circulated by a court official or:
   • A magazine article by a lady of the court who might have hoped for Miranda's position.

3 Make a note of each of the characters in the play who you consider has changed in the course of it. Write down where in the action the change has started to take place, and where any real transformation has been completed. Accompany your notes with brief quotations. Are there any characters who have not changed at all?

4 'This thing of darkness I Acknowledge mine' says Prospero of Caliban (lines 275–276). Assuming that he is not just saying that Caliban is his servant, but is recognising a darker side to his own nature, write a considered character study of Prospero, using quotations where relevant.

Explorations

What is *The Tempest* about?

The play deals with the resolution of a crisis – a crisis which struck twelve years previously and which Prospero has brooded on with recurrent memories of the terrors of the open sea and with recurrent bouts of fury. We know about the brooding; it comes tumbling out in his story to Miranda, and the fury is easily aroused at the sight of Ferdinand, a princely courtier such as his brother once was. On the island he has lived a life of privation – we have Caliban's recital of the food and drink that enabled them to exist, all secured with great effort. We could say that the original crisis has turned into what might today be called a 'mid-life crisis'. His life both in Milan and on the island has been wasted. All he has to show for it is some 'rough magic' and a pretty daughter, so what next?

By the beginning of the play, Prospero's studies in the occult have ripened to the point where he can use it to avenge the terrible wrong done to him and to Miranda. We are never sure quite how powerful his magic is – did he bring the ship to the island or just cause it to run aground when it got there? The stage direction in Act 3 *'Prospero on the top, invisible'* is a keynote of the play. Even before we know there is such a person as Prospero, the boatswain is telling Alonso and Antonio *'You mar our labour...You do assist the storm'* (Act 1 scene 1 lines 12–13). They do indeed, it is their presence and Prospero's *'on the top invisible'* which make it certain there will be a wreck. We only know this in retrospect; our viewpoint swivels to and fro, our sympathies come and go.

Prospero is in a position to destroy his enemies, but the very magic which has made this possible, makes it unlikely, even impossible. His inventiveness, his love of spectacle, even his association with Ariel seem to rule out a bloody ending. His magic is control, control over others' minds, emotions and actions, and over his own. We should be just as dismayed as Ferdinand over

Prospero's loss of control at the end of the masque; we would be if we had not observed this new threat for ourselves: the drunken bumbling, the plans which are way beyond their capacity to carry them out, the excited shopping-list of ways to murder Prospero.

The question is not whether the villains will be killed. We have seen Prospero prevent a double murder, and have heard his talk of providence, blessing and destiny in what can be seen as a Christian context. The problem is how it will all be resolved. There is not time for the characters to grow and develop. Prospero has had twelve years on the island, removed from his 'normal' context, they have had an afternoon. Alonso has had a shock and a sense of sustained loss, perhaps also a realisation that people are more important than things, but has his character changed? Perhaps the one-line reference to Antonio's son (Act 1 scene 2 line 436) is an indication that he was once to be treated in the same way. As it is, he remains fixed in his wickedness.

Prospero has brought his 'art' to the island. While in some contexts this means his 'magic', it is also the results of his studies. Prospero, an intelligent, educated and sensitive man brings to his new life the desire to educate others – his pupils are Miranda and Caliban. His belief is in the value of 'nurture' as opposed to basic 'nature'. Men and women do not become their true selves by nature alone, but by nurture. Prospero tells us about Miranda's education and their combined failure to improve the primitive Caliban. Miranda has become a 'wonder'; Caliban is still *'a thing most brutish', 'on whose nature nurture can never stick'*.

But in the real world, as in the dreamlike world of *The Tempest*, few people are all good or all bad. How has nurture adhered to Antonio? With all the advantages both of birth and upbringing he has no right to be not only a criminal but apparently incapable of improvement. Caliban on the other hand, with no chance – a dubious parentage and a scrappy education – shows more promise than Antonio and even seeks for *'grace'* when his wrongdoing is discovered.

Strangely, the final scene of the play is reminiscent of the final chapter in those country-house murder stories where everyone gathers in the library to hear 'whodunnit'. Prospero is able to tell: who didn't quite manage to kill him, who tried to kill two other people and who else planned to kill him. The other similarity is that you read this genre of writing for entertainment, and you go to the theatre for entertainment. The drama involves us in a story, provides a spectacle, sends out of the theatre an audience who are different in subtle ways from the people who went in. Just because we can read the text of the play as well as seeing it performed, it does not mean we should think that Shakespeare was writing a tract about nature versus nurture, or the evils of colonisation.

Interpretations

The Tempest is essentially a director's play. It needs to be seen and it offers an almost infinite number of possibilities. You have now read and studied the play. You have probably seen productions of it.

- How would you convey your understanding of it to a wider audience?
- Would you decide straightaway on a stage production? It is a stage play, after all.
- Would you perhaps prefer to look at other ideas, and try some lateral thinking?

Any complex play will present challenges to the director. You will have noticed some of them already.

A Imagine that you have decided to produce a television play or make a film of the *The Tempest*.

1 How would you deal with the long exposition, the story Prospero tells Miranda? Mime? Voice over? Flashback?
2 How could you make the best use of colour? Would the whole play be in colour? Realistic or stylised? What colours would you emphasise? Would you use monochrome? For which sections of the play?
3 How would you link the elements of the masque with what has been happening in the main play? Flashback? Inter-cutting? See Masque page 215.

B Imagine you have been asked to produce a radio play for people of your own age.

1 What are the problems likely to be? What are the opportunities?
2 Sound effects and music will obviously be even more important than in a stage version. Do you have any music in mind that might work?
3 What other uses could you make of the special qualities of sound drama?

C If you chose to produce a stage play of *The Tempest*, what aspects would you choose to emphasise?

1 Prospero is often on stage, but as observer not as an active participant. We have commented on *'Prospero, on the top, invisible'*. What do you think is the point of this? How could the idea of Prospero as a god-like figure, or a director within the play be developed in a production?
2 Another vital decision concerns how you would cast Prospero. He has traditionally been played as an old man, benign and bearded, but in fact he could well have married in his mid- to late-teens and Miranda is only 15. True, he may feel old at some points in the play, but what is the youngest he could be, bearing in mind that the mayhem in Milan would have taken some time to develop? What would be the effect of playing him as a younger man rather than as a benevolent old scholar?
3 Miranda is often played as an innocent and rather bland character. If you read her part closely, however, you might decide that she is only playing the part of a dutiful daughter and is actually far more lively. How do you see her?
4 Caliban and Ariel of course present really exciting possibilities. Prospero and the hidebound Italian courtiers perhaps see Caliban as 'deformed'. Is he, or is he just 'different' from them? How would you suggest this? How would you cast Ariel:
   • male or a female?
   • a dancer?
   • a mime artist?
   • an acrobat?
   • or ...
Consider some of these ideas and let them help to suggest some of your own. Discuss your ideas.

Drama activities

In the Activities sections we suggest a number of ways in which you can explore the play using drama. The notes that follow explain how the different types of activity can be organised. Most of the suggestions in the book fall into one of these groups:
- improvisation
- hotseating
- stopping the action
- forum theatre.

Improvisation

Improvisation is a form of theatre in which the actors do not have a written script, but make it up as they 'go along'. When you improvise, you need to know:
- **who** you are
- **when** and **where** the scene takes place
- **what** happened before the scene takes place
- **why** the scene is happening (for example if there is a conflict between the characters or a problem they are faced with).

How you improvise depends on how much planning and polishing you want to do. Some people like just to launch into the situation without any planning at all. This is a good way of working if you want to find out about the characters, relationships and emotions involved. Others like to discuss the situation and the main things that will happen before they begin to improvise. This is useful if you are working towards a scene, so that it becomes more confident and 'polished' – especially if you are preparing for a performance. Which approach you use depends on the situation you are working on and what you want to get out of it.

Hotseating

This is a good way of examining very closely the thoughts and feelings of one character at a key moment in the play.

For example, you might choose Prospero at the moment
when he accuses Ferdinand of being a spy. If you wanted
to explore this situation through hotseating, this is what
you would do:

1   Choose one member of the group to be Prospero.
2   That person sits 'in the hot seat', with the rest of the
    group around him.
3   Other members of the group ask Prospero about
    how he feels and why he acted in the way that he
    did.
4   Prospero must reply in character, and without
    pausing too long to think about his answer.
5   The rest of the group keep the questions going,
    picking up the replies that Prospero gives.
6   At the end you can discuss what came out of the
    questioning and whether Prospero's replies agree
    with the way other people see his character.

Variations

* The people in the group can become characters
  themselves: Ferdinand, Miranda, Ariel, Caliban and
  Alonso. Then each one has to ask questions from
  the point of view of that character.
* The questioners can take on different styles of
  questioning. One might be sympathetic, while a
  second would be aggressive, and a third sneering, for
  example.

Stopping the action

This is a different way of focusing on a particular moment
in the play. Instead of choosing a particular character,
you choose a particular moment. There are two main
ways in which you can do this.

Photographs

A photograph is based on the idea that you freeze a
particular moment in the play. You can do it in different
ways:

- Have one member in the group as the photographer. The rest of the group act the scene and at the moment the photographer says 'Freeze!', everyone must stay absolutely still.
- Choose the moment in the scene you want to photograph. Discuss how the photograph should look and then take up the positions you have agreed.
- Choose the moment in the scene you want to photograph. Give each member of the group a number. Number 1 takes up position as his/her character and freezes. Number 2 then joins Number one and freezes. Number 3 does the same and so on until everyone is in the photograph.

Once you have made your photograph you can come out of it one at a time and make suggestions about how it could be improved. You can also build on the photograph by one of the following:

- Make up a caption for the photograph.
- Let each character speak his or her thoughts at that moment in the play.

Statues/Paintings

For these you choose one member of the group to be the artist. Then choose:

- a moment in the play
- a title you have made up
- a quotation.

The artist then arranges the members of the group, one by one into a group statue of the chosen subject. Different members of the group can take it in turn to be the artist.

Forum theatre

Another way of exploring a key moment in the play is called 'forum theatre'. The group divides in two:

- A small number of actors to take on roles
- The rest, are theatre directors.

You then work as follows:

1   Chose the moment in the play you are going to work on. (For example, the moment in Act 4 scene 1 when Caliban says, 'we now are near his cell'.)

2   Choose someone to be Caliban.

3   Arranging the space you are working in, agree where the characters are, where people enter and exit and so on.

4   Start by asking Caliban to say what he thinks about where he should be and how he should move.

5   Then the rest of the group, the 'directors', try out different ways of presenting that moment. For example:
    • they can ask him to speak his lines in a particular way
    • they can suggest he uses certain moves or gestures.

6   The short extract from the play can be tried in several different ways until the group have used up all the ideas.

7   Then you should discuss what worked and what didn't work and why.

Character

Characters in plays function in two ways:

1 They have to be written and acted in such a way that the audience (or reader) can imagine them to have a life of their own; the audience wants to make the characters 'live'.
2 They are part of the writer's overall plan – that is, they do not, in fact, have a life of their own but are the writer's tools for exploring their themes in life-like form.

N.B. Questions about character are common in A-level, but they cannot best be answered by writing a character analysis (however complex) as though they were a 'real' human being. The aim should be to explain why this complex creation is essential to the play as a whole; this is the best literary writing.

Three lines of approach

Judging a character is not simply a matter of accumulating the evidence of the written word and drawing conclusions. It is more complicated, and requires some selection and evaluation to allow you to reach a coherent response to the character.

The evidence – 1

Characters are revealed by:
- what they say
- what they do.

Problems

1 Unfortunately (for examination purposes) characters are not always consistent. Major characters are subject to change because the events on which the action is based are significant enough to affect the main protagonists: the more important the character, the closer to the action and the greater the reaction to events.

You must always be aware of how, and why, characters are developing and be prepared to explain and trace the changes.

2 Characters might say or do things for effect. They might be seeking to impress or mislead someone else and not mean what they say at all.

You must always consider whether the character is being sincere or if they have an ulterior motive.

The evidence – 2

Characters are also revealed by:
- what others say about them
- how others behave towards them.

Problems

As in life, whether you accept A's opinion of B depends on how you feel about A. If you believe that A is untrustworthy or has a perverted sense of justice, then A's criticism of B might be interpreted as a glowing character reference! Alternatively, an opinion might be based on false information or might be deliberately misleading.

It is essential that you do not simply accept one character's opinion of another at face value.

The evidence – 3

Characters are also revealed by:
- soliloquies
- asides.

These are often the most reliable evidence on which to assess a character since they are sharing their thoughts with the audience. All pretence is dropped because the soliloquy and the aside are devices which allow characters to express their thoughts and feelings directly, and solely, to the audience.

Critical moments

At critical moments in the play you can begin to gain a better insight into a character by seeking answers to certain questions. There is no formula which will apply to every situation, but you need to identify the key scenes and speeches which relate to a particular character and then ask these questions to start you off and perhaps prompt questions of your own.

- What has the character said or done here?
- Why has the character said or done this?
- What will happen as a result of this speech or action?
- How do you feel about the consequences of this speech or action?
- What does this incident tell us about the character?
- How does the character change or develop as a result of it?

What does each of these critical moments tell us about the character concerned?

Caliban

The character in *The Tempest* who best demonstrates this approach is Caliban. He is also, unexpectedly, probably the character who changes most in the brief course of the play. We learn about him from hearsay (from two characters who have no sympathy with him at all); from his speeches to them and theirs to him; from him when he is alone; from two servant characters who unexpectedly encounter him; from his plot; from his desire for pardon.

We see him first through Prospero's and Miranda's eyes. Investigate and find quotations for what has formed their opinions, or fuelled their prejudices. Look at:

- Caliban's parentage
- the way Caliban speaks to them – they see him as a thing, not as a sentient being
- his attempted violation of Miranda
- their conviction that by his very nature he cannot be made good
- the ease with which Prospero can verbally abuse and torment him.

You should be aware of these points:

1 A stage representation or your own mental picture of him will inevitably colour your attitude.
2 Miranda's and Prospero's 'evidence' may be tainted.
3 Is he 'deformed' or just 'different'?

4 Can a man be guilty of rape when his own culture has no concept of it?

5 It is very easy to impose your 'modern' liberal views on a play written four centuries ago.

Once Caliban speaks at length, decide and show by quotation, whether he:

- has grounds for resentment
- did respond differently to them at first
- helped them survive
- is too severely punished
- is mentally and physically hurt.

If Act 1 shows us what we may expect of this character, Act 2 starts to show us what life is like for him. We learn this from:

- his soliloquy
- his reaction to other people
- his reaction to apparent kindness
- his ability to project hopes (however misguided) for a better life.

In Act 3 scene 2, although he is drunk, certain clear characteristics come through. List them, with references.

- Pay attention to what Caliban says about the island and what this speech tells us about him.

Caliban's main task, in dramatic terms, is to replicate Prospero's original fate, but note how he plans it. In Act 4 Prospero, alone, speaks again about Caliban:

- Has Prospero's opinion changed?

Caliban seems more sober than Trinculo and Stephano:

- Can you suggest reasons for this?
- Why is Caliban not distracted by the things which lure the other two?
- Why is he so focused?

In Act 5 does Caliban's final speech tell us anything new about him?

A similar approach can be used for Antonio, Gonzalo, and to a lesser extent for Alonso, Sebastian, Ferdinand and Miranda. Prospero, however, seems to be much more elusive.

Prospero

Prospero has organised the shipwreck and implies he must seize this moment if his fortunes are to change. Thus the arrival of his enemies is the catalyst he has been planning for, and their arrival precipitates the action which follows – almost like a chemical reaction.

We have:

- Prospero's narrative, the exposition
- the way he speaks to and about Miranda
- his dealings with Caliban and Ariel
- the arranged marriage for Miranda (or for his own purposes?)
- his soliloquies and asides
- the critical moment when he decides to forgive…or did Ariel decide it for him?

With this last point we come to the unknown area. Since much of what we learn about Prospero's intentions and attitudes is discovered from his instructions to Ariel, is Ariel part of his character? Is it perhaps a part he has only been able to develop on the island? Is Caliban then a part of him too, '*this thing of darkness*'. Is this why he hates him so much? It could be that this is where we have to look, through the magic and the hatred to find the complete Prospero.

The language of the play

Shakespeare was an expert scriptwriter. Apart from essential stage directions, most of the clues the actors need in order to create their characters are in the language, and not merely in the meaning, but in the form, the style, and the imagery.

You will have been aware of the variety of different styles within the play. The main categories are blank verse, prose and rhyming verse (see GLOSSARY on pages 224, 225 and 226 for simple definitions).

Blank verse is the most prevalent style in the play. As a medium it can be monotonous, particularly if the sense of a line is regularly concluded at the end of the line. Shakespeare took blank verse, and especially in his later plays, made it an instrument of amazing versatility and beauty. Look for instance at Caliban's lines in Act 3 scene 2 lines 138–144. You can make yourself thump out the mechanical beat, but when you read it, preferably aloud, for sense, the effect is altogether different, but still underpinned by the rhythm. The pause is often in the middle of the line, or the sense may run on without a pause for two or three lines.

Blank verse: close study

Look in more detail at Antonio's speeches to Sebastian in Act 2 scene 1. Study and speak lines 240–248. Antonio is in a hurry – he doesn't know how soon the others will wake up. He also has to persuade Sebastian to a course of action. Notice how:
- 'she' is repeated in lines 240, 241, 244 and takes a stress
- the pause is only once placed at the end of a line
- the exaggerations are memorable, and help persuade (lines 241, 243 and 244)
- dashes effectively put brackets round one exaggeration he's only just thought up
- the alliteration in lines 241–242, 243, 244, 245 and 247 enhances the argument
- the rushing list comes to an end with two and a half sober lines, with the rhythm of the last line finished by the first part of Sebastian's reply.

Prose

We have already looked at the use of prose at the very beginning of the play, for urgent action and panic. Where else is it used, and for what reasons?

Rhymed verse

Look too at the rhyme patterns of the songs in the masque as well as the rhyming couplets of the goddesses' speeches, where the length of the line and the recurrent rhyme give weight to what they say.

Ariel's songs tend to use a shorter line. What effect does this have in helping to establish his role? Ariel ends Act 2 scene 1 with a rhyming couplet, a device which in *A Midsummer Night's Dream*, for example, is used to assure us that however serious the subject matter, there will not be a tragic ending.

Imagery

Imagery is always closely allied with the themes and atmosphere of the play. Look at the theme of punishment. Prospero, always in control, feels that he needs to punish, or threaten punishment, to keep both his servants in order. Even Ferdinand does not escape. Torture, and the fear of it, was in Shakespeare's time one of the state's instruments of control.

In Act 1 scene 2 lines 280–281 Prospero reminds Ariel of past torment, the release from which has bound Ariel to him in unwilling gratitude:

> '...left thee there, where thou didst vent thy groans
> As fast as mill-wheels strike'

In the same scene lines 287–289   'thy groans
> Did make wolves howl, and penetrate the breasts
> Of ever-angry bears'

He threatens Caliban (lines 326–329):
> 'Side-stitches that shall pen thy breath up.
> ....thou shalt be pinched
> As thick as honeycomb...'

Follow through these examples on the same subject:
> Act 2 scene 2 lines 6–12
> Act 4 scene 1 lines 257–260.

Explore the following groups of imagery, listing as many examples as you can find:
- sleep
- sea
- nature
- the elements
- illusion
- curses.

Action and dramatic structure

A play is constructed – that is to say the action is ordered and organised – to achieve two principal aims:

- To tell the story in a way that will keep the audience wanting to know more until the writer is ready to deliver the outcome.
- To explore and develop the themes the writer chooses to bring alive through the words, motives, actions and interactions of the characters.

It is helpful when considering the structure of *The Tempest* to carry out a straightforward mechanistic survey of the contents:

- count the number of text pages in each act and work out roughly what proportion of the play each occupies
- count the number of scenes in each act
- make a very brief note of the characters in each scene. This is best done as a table. Each character or group of characters forming the various story threads can even be coloured in. This will show you at a glance the weight and distribution of these storylines through the play.

When you have done all this, you can answer the following questions:

1 Which is the longest act, occupying more than a quarter of the play? Why? Is it conditioned by the plot? What effect does the relative weight of this act seem to have on the play as a whole?

2 How many of the main characters are introduced in Act 1?

3 What do you notice about Act 3, the central act in this five-act drama? Which of the plot elements are carried forward in this act?

4 When you have looked at the contents of Acts 4 and 5 what is your reaction?

Dramatic structure and patterns

If you have carried out the very simple exercise suggested above, you will have seen the pattern in which plots and sub-plots are managed. Every play of any complexity will seek to keep the audience wondering, its interest alive. In *The Tempest* there is an additional group of patterns; repetitive behaviour, either reported or taking place during the action of the play.

Under these headings, and using the line references, make a note of these patterns and the characters they involve:

1 Landings on the island

For example
- Act 1 scene 2 line 171
- Act 2 scene 2 line 122
- Act 5 scene 1 lines 215–218

There are many more references – see how many you can find.

2 Plots to kill

- Act 1 scene 2 lines 121–127
- Act 2 scene 1 lines 286–290
- Act 3 scene 2 lines 62–63

3 Plans to mate with, or marry, Miranda

- Act 1 scene 2 lines 344–347
- Act 1 scene 2 line 445
- Act 3 scene 2 lines 107–108

4 People exiled, confined, or prevented from moving

- Act 1 scene 2 lines 144–148
- Act 1 scene 2 line 270

Again, find more of your own.

5 People who have controlled the island, or would like to

- Act 1 scene 2 lines 331–332
- Act 5 scene 1 lines 159–162
- Act 2 scene 1 lines 139–141
- Act 2 scene 2 lines 175–176

Things to think about

1 The play, unusually, starts with people arriving in an alien environment. All the movement is inward. We are not sure until near the end that everyone who wants to leave will do so. For most of the play the island is a prison.

2 The characters are inevitably thrown in on themselves. Investigate how these repeated patterns have the almost dream-like quality of action replays. They reinforce our sensation of the constraint the characters are under.

3 They also serve to emphasise universal patterns in human behaviour. How might this be important for the themes of the play? Look for instance at your own reaction to:
   - people who thwart you
   - your desire to be somewhere else, even to start again
   - the position of women in society four centuries after Shakespeare was writing
   - your attitude to authority and to the way we are governed.

Contexts

When we watch contemporary drama of whatever sort in the theatre, the cinema or on television, we bring with us a vast amount of knowledge and possibly even direct experience. For four hundred years, directors of Shakespeare's plays have found contemporary relevance in the acting out of family conspiracies, political murders, racial and sexual discrimination. What about the groundlings of Shakespeare's day – what was their necessary background knowledge? We cannot know in any detail what news and ballad sheets were on the streets or what the gossip was at breakfast or dinner or in the taverns. We can sometimes see the broad strokes – the political situation, social attitudes and common beliefs. These can only be suggested here and the student will gain much personal satisfaction from wider reading and more extended research.

Historical and political contexts

Conspiracies

In March 1603, Elizabeth I, who had reigned for almost half a century, died. Shortly before her death she named as her successor 'My kinsman the King of Scots'. There was much public rejoicing that there was a peaceful change of ruler and James Stuart, James I of England and VI of Scotland (where he had ruled for many years) came to the throne. The first play presented for the King by Shakespeare's company, renamed *The King's Men* by James, was *Measure for Measure*. Although neither written nor produced for this specific purpose, the emphasis on justice and mercy tempering absolute power was likely to please the new monarch. How did *The Tempest*, probably written in 1610 or 1611, reflect contemporary interests? At this period royalty could scarcely rest secure. The possibility of counter claims to the throne or of conspiracy was often present, witness the discovery of the Gunpowder Plot in 1605. There are two conspiracies in *The Tempest*. How does Prospero deal with them? Why do you think Shakespeare gives a comic dimension to Caliban's conspiracy and how might the royal audience have reacted?

First performance

We know that an early performance of *The Tempest* took place at Court in Whitehall on 1st November 1611. We know that *The Tempest* was performed again, either late in 1612 or early in 1613 as one item in the elaborate festivities for the betrothal of James's only surviving daughter, the Princess Elizabeth, to Prince Frederick of Heidelberg, Elector of the Rhineland Palatinate. James's son, the popular Prince Henry, had recently died, and his father was hardly in festive mood. The wedding took place on St Valentine's Day 1613. This marriage essentially established a political alliance for James I, giving him an English base on the continent. This new Protestant alliance was most desirable as a counterbalance to the recently established treaty with Catholic Spain.

The 16th and early 17th centuries saw many daring voyages of exploration. The wooden sailing ships which sailed across the Atlantic were not much bigger than the fishing boats which today work in and out of the Channel ports. The early ships had few aids to navigation and no accurate charts to show reefs or rocks. They had to carry food, water and spars and rigging for repairs. They scarcely knew where or when their next landfall might be. The eastern seaboard of North America had been 'discovered' and a colony was established in Virginia in 1606. By 1609 the colony was in difficulties and a small fleet, commanded by Admiral Sir George Somers, set out with 500 settlers, men, women and children. In a fierce hurricane off the West Indies, Somers's ship went aground on the coast of the Bermudas which Somers instantly claimed for the British crown. Everyone survived, the ship did not break up, the island was delightful, there was abundant food and they rescued plenty of stores from the ship. Eventually two smaller ships could be built and they reached Virginia.

This seemed little short of miraculous. Letters from survivors and official accounts of the voyage reached London, and of course the news reached Shakespeare's audiences. Shakespeare himself will have read the original accounts, and may even have known some of the people involved in the venture.

Social attitudes and beliefs

The noble savage

The Bermudas were uninhabited, but elsewhere the indigenous people were viewed by the colonisers with a mixture of curiosity, condescension and fear. Like Caliban they had their uses at first and then were used; or they fell victim to the use of guns, to previously unknown diseases or to drink, or they turned on their oppressors. Captain Smith, an early coloniser in Virginia, was captured by an Indian chief and owed his life to the pleas of the chief's daughter, Pocahontas. Caliban's cry 'This island's mine, by Sycorax, my mother' desperately insists on a right of succession, which a Jacobean audience would have recognised, and not the 'finders keepers' attitude of Propero.

Montaigne was a French philosopher and essayist who lived from 1533 to 1592. In his essay 'On Cannibals' he wrote about the unspoilt South American Indian before he was subjected to the 'civilising' influence of Europeans. In Gonzalo's speech describing what he would do with the island, Shakespeare borrows heavily from the Montaigne essay. The golden age which Montaigne evokes is not, of course, one capable of being imposed upon people who have been used to a completely different lifestyle. Sebastian and Antonio deride this vision and we cannot know whether Shakespeare's own attitude favoured theirs or Gonzalo's or Montaigne's. We know that Montaigne had met three Brazilian Indians, and Trinculo makes it clear (Act 2 scene 2) that dead Indians had been exhibited as a sideshow at fairs. What impact might Shakespeare's depiction of Caliban have had on his audience? How have present-day directors in productions you have seen chosen to portray him? What is your reaction to this character?

Magic and witchcraft

From the start of the play to the moment when Prospero breaks his staff and 'drowns his book' we are entertained by magic. He claims that his magic has been stronger than that wielded by Sycorax. Before the play starts Sycorax has been banished from Algiers and cast away. In addition to terrible sorceries committed there, she has allegedly mated with the devil to produce her son. Belief in witchcraft was widespread and agonising 'tests' for women suspected of witchcraft often ended in the death of the woman, whether she was 'proved' innocent or guilty. While in Scotland, James had become obsessed for a while with witchcraft, and during the trial of the 'witches of North Berwick' had apparently questioned the women himself. In 1597 he had written a treatise on demonology.

Both the Roman Catholic and Protestant religions condemned magic and witchcraft as evil and the theory of demonology attributed witches' powers to their special links with the devil, especially their sexual relationship with him. There is no suggestion of any pact with the devil in Prospero's case. Towards the end of the play he declares his intention of destroying the trappings of sorcery and, having presumably done so off stage, in the epilogue he finally puts his faith in prayer and relies on mercy, just as he has granted mercy to those who wronged him. Although not specifically mentioned here, Prospero and his audience will have been very much aware of the idea of possible punishment in an afterlife for wrongs committed in this one.

Dramatic context

Shakespeare's theatre

We have mostly assumed that the words of Shakespeare's plays are not to be trifled with. The idea tends to be that Shakespeare wrote them and that he knew best. The texts have become sacrosanct.

When the plays were in performance 400 years ago, things were very different. An actor would have only his own part written out for him; he would not have access to the whole text. The danger in having the whole play available to read was that of pirated editions. If the play was successful then others would want to put it on. As the plays eventually came to be written down, scribes would insert their own memories of performances they had seen and bits of stage business they had appreciated. Copying and recopying produced errors – it always does. *The Tempest* was not published until 1623, in the First Folio edition, as the first play in the collection. The acts and scenes were marked and detailed stage directions given. This is considered to be a good text, set up by Ralph Crane, a professional scribe and copyist, careful of correct punctuation, possibly from a version used in the production of the play.

Another point to consider is that Shakespeare's actors formed in effect a repertory company; they would have been known to regular members of the audience who would recognise and greet them in each fresh role. The temptation in the comic scenes to play to the audience must have been irresistible.

It is tempting to imagine where such an improvisation might have happened. We know that *The Tempest* formed part of the celebrations for the wedding of James I's daughter. On the South Bank of the Thames across from Whitehall where the performance took place, a model of the city of Algiers was erected. There were also exciting and originally designed firework displays, including one where squibs shaped like hounds chased a deer through the air, with much realistic detail. It is probably merely coincidence, but it could just be that Shakespeare was adding contemporary allusions (the 'spirit' pack of hounds chasing Caliban and the others at the end of Act 4). In the case of Ariel's reply to Prospero's question about where Sycorax was born ('Sir, in Argier') the actor may even have improvised a topical comment with a nod across the river – especially as it seems temporarily to 'throw' Prospero.

The unities

Asked the time in Act 1 scene 2, Ariel says 'Past the mid season'. Prospero replies 'At least two glasses. The time 'twixt six and now Must by us both be spent most preciously'. In Act 5 the boatswain remarks that 'Our ship, Which but three glasses since, we gave out split, Is tight and yare'. So the action of *The Tempest* is very tightly conceived – it does not just take place within twenty-four hours, but within the 'real time' of the performance. Since a 'glass' at sea is half an hour, the play would seem to occupy rather more time than the events it portrays.

You could argue that *The Tempest* is written within the general 'rules' of the three unities. These formed a theory of dramatic composition from the writings of Aristotle, a Greek scholar, teacher and writer, who lived in the fourth century BC. He said that a drama should have unity of action (only one plot) and unity of time (it should all take place in the same time it took to perform). Later writers added unity of place (the action should have only one setting). The theory was thought to concentrate the attention on the central events of the drama. It had much more effect on the French playwrights of the seventeenth century than on English drama.

The unities are not a theory to which Shakespeare normally paid much attention: his plays frequently have one or more subplots and sometimes cover many years in their action, with settings widely dispersed. In *The Tempest* he used unities of time and place; some would argue that he observed unity of action as well. This may have been deliberate or accidental. What effects, positive or negative, do you think this has on the structure of *The Tempest*?

Masque

The masque was originally an amateur entertainment involving masks and disguise. As early as the fourteenth century a group of friends, bearing torches and wearing masks would pay an unexpected visit to a house and dance for the host and hostess and their guests. At the end of the organised dancing, the spectators would be invited to join in. By the fifteenth century, the action involved mime and spectacle, and these 'disguisings' became more of a show put on for the spectators – actors with an audience.

In Elizabeth I's reign, masques became extravagant spectacles, combining acting, mime allegorical pageantry and elaborately constructed and decorated scenery and fantastic costumes.

Under James I and his queen, the masque rapidly developed into one of the most popular court entertainments. As the dramatic element became more important, playwrights and designers were commissioned. Although fabulously expensive and elaborate, the masque was often still only the prelude to the revels, dancing and other entertainments of the evening.

Some directors have found the masque in *The Tempest* difficult to deal with and a critic has described it as 'rather perfunctory' and 'scarcely necessary'. We should therefore try to decide why Shakespeare included it. In addition to being a spectacular entertainment, the court masque was designed to praise the monarch and to proclaim his power and his moral virtues.

You should think about these points:

- The union of Ferdinand and Miranda will prevent future rivalry and nastiness between Milan and Naples – a tribute to statesmanlike planning. Cupid, with his alleged involvement in the abduction of Ceres' daughter, will not be present in the masque.
- The happy future of the engaged couple is foretold by the symbolic absence of winter in their lives.
- The hardships and privations endured on the island will soon be only a memory, and Prospero will shortly abandon his sorcery. This is symbolically replaced in the masque by the stately vision of an eternally sunlit and ordered countryside and a more tranquil future. Does this seem to you to be a representation of the Italian countryside with which the (limited) audience would be familiar?
- After this last joyful demonstration of his magical powers, Prospero prepares to lay them down. There is inevitably in this vision of the future a sense that he is looking ahead to passing on the ducal powers he will have resumed to his daughter and son-in-law.

Possible sources for The Tempest

1 There is no one clear source for the plot, just elements in plays or scenarios already existing which may or may not have influenced Shakespeare.

2 A play called *Die schöne Sidea* (Fair Sidea) by a minor German dramatist Jakob Ayrer, who died in 1605, tells of a prince who is a magician with control over a spirit, and a daughter with whom his enemy's son falls in love. He is made to carry logs and his sword too is paralysed by magic. But there is no tempest and no island. It is possible, of course, that there may have been a now-unknown earlier source for both plays.

3 One of the Commedia dell'arte scenarios called *Li Tre Satiri*, which Shakespeare just might have seen enacted by an Italian troupe visiting England, featured a shipwreck, an island and a magician. There were islanders who thought the crew were gods and the clown stole the magician's book.

   The Commedia dell'arte was an Italian theatrical form which flourished throughout Europe from the 16th to the 18th century. It was far more popular in mainland Europe than in England – most of the verbal humour in dialect form would be lost on a foreign audience – and consequently it had less influence here on mainstream theatre than, for example, in France, in the work of Molière. Essentially popular theatre, it featured ensemble playing, improvisation, easily recognisable stock characters and situations, and masks. Shakespeare's comic scenes certainly incorporate some of the Commedia dell'arte devices and atmosphere.

4 There was also a real-life Prospero in fifteenth-century Italy, a Duke of Genoa who was deposed.

5 A travel book by Richard Eden, published in 1577, gives Setebos as a Patagonian god.

Themes

If a play is good, its themes will not seem abstract or theoretical because they will be seen in the form of 'real' issues in the 'lives' of the characters, and will be explored through parallel and contrasting experiences.

Look at these themes, and the way in which they are worked out:

- control
- obedience
- exile, confinement, containment
- treachery
- punishment
- forgiveness
- latent sexuality.

Preparing for an examination

You will be expected to have a detailed and accurate knowledge of your set texts. You must have read your set texts several times and you need to know the sequence of events and the narrative. The plot summaries in this edition will help you with this. You will get little credit in the final examination for merely 'telling the story', and simply 'going through' the narrative is seen as particularly worthless in an open-book examination. However, you will not be able to argue a convincing case or develop a deep understanding unless you have this detailed knowledge as a basis.

The questions

A-level questions are demanding but they should always be accessible and central, a fair test of your knowledge and understanding. They are rarely obscure or marginal. There is actually a relatively small number of questions which can be asked on any text, even though the ways in which they can be worded are almost infinite. They tend to fall into quite straightforward categories or types, as outlined below.

Character

You may be asked to discuss your response to a particular character, to consider the function or presentation of a character or perhaps to compare and contrast characters.

Society

You may be asked to consider the kind of society depicted by the text or perhaps the way in which individuals relate to that society.

Themes

You may be asked to discuss the ideas and underlying issues which are explored by a text, and what are the author's concerns and interests.

Attitudes

You may be asked to consider what views or values are revealed by the text, what is valued and what is attacked.

Style or technique

You may be asked to look at the methods a writer uses to achieve particular effects. In essence, you are being asked to examine 'how' a text achieves its effects and you need to consider such matters as diction, imagery, tone and structure.

Personal response

You may be asked to give your own view of the text but this must be more than just unsupported assertion. You need to move beyond 'I think...' to a well-considered evaluation based on close reading and textual evidence. It is worth remembering that there is not an infinity of sensible responses to a text.

'Whole text' questions

These questions require you to consider the text as a whole. You need a coherent overview of the text and the ability to select appropriate detail and evidence.

'Specific' passages

These questions require close reading and analysis but sometimes the specific passage has to be related to another passage or perhaps to the whole text.

Writing an essay

A critical essay attempts to construct a clear argument based on the evidence of the text. It needs a clear sense of direction and purpose and it is better to start with a simple, coherent attitude than to ramble aimlessly or produce a shapeless answer. Each paragraph should be a step in a developing argument and be supported by textual detail which is relevant to the question. You must answer the question set – as opposed to the question you wanted to be set. You must be prepared to discuss a specific aspect of the text or approach it from a slightly new or unexpected angle. You will need to be selective in your choice of material appropriate to the actual question. An essay which deals only in sweeping generalisations can lack detail and substance. One which gets too involved in minor details may lack direction and a conceptual framework. You need to combine an overview and detailed knowledge.

Although different examination boards and syllabuses have their own ways of expressing them, there are basically three criteria against which your work will be judged. They are:
- knowledge and understanding
- answering the question relevantly
- written expression.

Essay questions

1 Why is the play called *The Tempest* and not, for example, *The Enchanted Island* or *The Magician*?
2 Investigate the suggestion that magic serves as a short cut to characterisation and plotting in *The Tempest*.
3 Compare Prospero and Alonso as rulers and as desert island exiles.
4 How convinced are we at the end of the play that Alonso has changed?
5 It has been claimed that the structure of the play is at the same time enabling and restrictive. Illustrate both sides of this statement.

6 'Prospero has found in his exile a close encounter with his own person – body and appetite in the form of Caliban, his imagination and creation in Ariel.' Discuss.

7 Would you agree that Miranda and Claribel are both chattels of their father, there to serve political and territorial ends, and that love doesn't come into it?

8 Are Stephano and Trinculo lovable rogues or villains?

9 Is Gonzalo the one truly good character in the play?

10 'It is a sad reflection on human nature that every character in *The Tempest* is out for their own advantage.' Do you agree?

11 Has Ariel any personality of his own, or is he just a convenient figment of Prospero's (and Shakespeare's) imagination?

12 Throughout the play we are constantly reminded that we are on an island. How is this done?

13 The masque is unnecessary and even disruptive. What purpose does it serve?

14 'Caliban is the ground of the play. His function is to illuminate by contrast the world of art, nurture, and civility.' Discuss.

15 For twelve years Prospero has been on a journey of discovery. In the final Act he reaches his destination. What does he discover and where has he arrived?

16 What does Gonzalo mean when he says in Act 5 *'and all of us (found) ourselves When no man was his own'*?

17 Would you agree that Prospero shows true nobility only when he renounces vengeance for forgiveness?

Glossary

Alliteration: A figure of speech in which a number of words close to each other in a piece of writing begin with the same sound. Alliteration helps to draw attention to the words.
'Full fathom five thy father lies'
(Act 1 scene 2 line 395)
In another example:
'Tis as impossible that he's undrowned
As he that sleeps here swims'
(Act 2 scene 1 lines 231–232)
In addition to the alliteration, the same 's' sound is repeated internally (in 'impossible'), and also finally (in '*'Tis*', '*as*' '*sleeps*' and '*swims*'). This emphasizes the hissing effect in this conspiratorial speech.

Antithesis: A figure of speech in which the writer brings two opposite or contrasting ideas up against each other.

ANTONIO: *'Thou let'st thy fortune sleep – die rather; winks't*
               Whiles thou art waking.'
(Act 2 scene 1 lines 210–211)

Apostrophe: When a character suddenly speaks directly to someone or something, which may or may not be present:
'Thou poisonous slave, got by the devil himself
Upon thy wicked dam, come forth!'
(Act 1 scene 2 lines 319–320)
and
'Mistress line, is not this my jerkin?'
(Act 4 scene 1 line 234–235)

Aside: A speech which can be long or, more usually, short, made by one of the characters for the ears of the audience alone, or for the benefit of another, named character. As with a soliloquy (see page 220) we rely on an aside to express the true feelings of the character.

                    'No, pray thee.
(Aside) I must obey. His art is of such power,
It would control my dam's god Setebos
And make a vassal of him.'
(Act 1 scene 2 lines 371–374)

Assonance: The repetition of vowel sounds within words in a line, sometimes for poetic effect or to reinforce a point, or, as here, both:
'His tears run down his beard like winter's drops
From eaves of reeds.'
(Act 5 scene 1 lines 16–17)

Blank verse: Verse which does not rhyme and in which each line has ten syllables comprising five 'feet', or measures, of two syllables each. Each foot consists of a short (weak) syllable, followed by a long (strong) syllable. This is known as an iambus. Since there are five to a line, the line is known as the iambic pentameter.

Double meaning: see *Pun*.

Dramatic irony: A situation in a play when the audience (and possibly some of the characters) knows something that one or more of the characters does not:
'He does hear me
And that he does, I weep. Myself am Naples,'
(Act 1 scene 2 lines 431–432)

Epilogue: A speech at the end of the play summing it up and commenting on it; also the character who delivers such a speech.

Hendiadys: A figure of speech expressed by two nouns joined by 'and'.
'In the dark backward and abysm of time'
(Act 1 scene 2 line 50)
for 'In the dark, earlier abysm of time'

Hyperbole: Deliberate exaggeration, for dramatic effect.
'You are gentlemen of brave mettle; you would lift the moon out of her sphere...'
(Act 2 scene 1 lines 176–178). This same sentence also contains an example of irony and punning.

Irony: When someone says one thing and means another.
'Foolish wench,
To the most of men this is a Caliban
And they to him are angels.'
(Act 1 scene 2 lines 477–479)

There can be irony in actions as well as words. In Act 2 scene 2, Caliban again, this time voluntarily, becomes a servant. The irony lies in the fact that this time he is not even a servant to a man who started by wishing him well and hoping to teach him, but to a drunken butler whose first reaction was to carry him off to make money out of him.

Onomatopoeia: Using words that are chosen because they mimic the sound of what is being described:

'All wound with adders, who with cloven tongues
Do hiss me into madness.'
(Act 2 scene 2 lines 13–14)
Also the refrain to Ariel's song in Act 1 scene 2 lines 401–402:
'Ding dong.
Hark, now I hear them – Ding-dong bell.'

Oxymoron: A figure of speech in which the writer combines two ideas which are opposites. This frequently has a startling or unusual effect.

'to sigh
To the winds whose pity, sighing back again
Did us but loving wrong.'
(Act 1 scene 2 lines 149–151)

Personification: Referring to a thing or an idea as if it were a person:
'Methought the billows spoke and told me of it,
The winds did sing it to me; and the thunder,
That deep and dreadful organ-pipe, pronounced
The name of Prosper.'
(Act 3 scene 3 lines 96-99)

Play on words: see *Pun*.

Prose: In some scenes, characters' speeches are not written in verse but in 'ordinary' sentences – prose. Shakespeare often uses it for workpeople or servants, but this is far from being an absolute rule. Caliban for instance uses both blank verse and prose, and this is only partly dependent on the company he is in.

Pun: A figure of speech in which the writer uses a word that has more than one meaning, or a word which has the same sound as one which has another meaning:

GONZALO: *when every grief is entertained*
                                  That's offered, comes to th' entertainer –
SEBASTIAN: *A dollar*
GONZALO: *Dolour comes to him indeed*
(Act 2 scene 1 lines 16–19)

Rhetorical question: A question which does not expect an answer, or which the speaker is about to answer for effect. In a play it can often provide information or give a background which as a statement might sound awkward, tedious or pedantic.
                          'When we were boys,
Who would believe that there were mountaineers
Dew-lapped like bulls, whose throats had hanging at 'em
Wallets of flesh?'
(Act 3 scene 3 lines 43–46)
Here it becomes a stage direction embedded in the text:
    'shrug'st thou, malice?'
(Act 1 scene 2 line 367)

Rhymed verse: Sometimes Shakespeare uses a pattern of rhymed lines. This can be simply two successive lines (a rhyming couplet) to round off a scene or an incident within a scene. Sometimes whole speeches will rhyme as in the masque, for special emphasis.

Soliloquy: Spoken apparently to himself or herself when a character is alone on stage, or separated from the other characters in some way. In *The Tempest* only the audience observes Ferdinand reconciling himself to the task Prospero has set, Caliban telling us what mental and physical torments he has to undergo and Prospero giving up his magic.

Unities, the: A theory of dramatic composition derived from the writings of Aristotle, a Greek scholar, teacher and writer living in the third century BC. They are
  1 Unity of action: one main plot
  2 Unity of time: events take place in 24 hours or less
  3 Unity of place: one setting
(See page 214 for relevance to *The Tempest*.)